M⁵

★ ★
FOUR
DAYS IN
PHILADELPHIA
1776

★★
FOUR
DAYS IN
PHILADELPHIA
1776

By Mary Kay Phelan

Illustrated by Charles Walker

973.3
Ph

#27091

THOMAS Y. CROWELL COMPANY   NEW YORK

BY THE AUTHOR

Mother's Day
The Fourth of July
Election Day
Four Days in Philadelphia—1776

Designed by SALLIE BALDWIN

Manufactured in the United States of America
L.C. Card 67–18521

3 4 5 6 .7 8 9 10

To my favorite critics . . .
MARTY, JERRY, EDNA, and DICK

CONTENTS

★ ★
FOUR
DAYS IN
PHILADELPHIA
1776

The First of July

★★ *1* ★★

WHILE THE COCK CROWS

Although it is early—still quite early—in the city of Philadelphia on this morning of July 1, 1776, the air seems charged with a sense of suppressed excitement. Only the fifty-odd members of the Second Continental Congress are fully aware of the monumental question which will be presented to the delegation at the State House today. Yet for weeks "the City of Brotherly Love" has been alive with rumors.

Passersby have eavesdropped on heated conversations as the delegates emerged from their meeting room at Fifth and Chestnut. Hints have been overheard around the tables at City Tavern over on Second Street where the members often gather after strenuous sessions. All this has been the basis for

3

widespread gossip. The people of Philadelphia haven't been able to pinpoint anything with certainty—all meetings of the Congress are held behind closed doors, of course. But everyone seems to sense that something important is about to happen.

The secrecy of the sessions follows a precedent established more than two years ago at the initial gathering of the First Continental Congress. Even then, the distinguished delegates recognized that with so many diverse opinions about England and each other, conflict was inevitable. Undoubtedly among themselves there would be bitter and furious debate. Yet all agreed that—to the outside world—a show of unanimity must be presented.

Though voices might be raised and fists shaken, the members of Congress resolved that no hint of argument should escape the confines of the meeting room. Each delegate was pledged not to divulge either actions or conversations taking place on the floor. As a result, the proceedings have never been published; not one dissenting voice has been recorded in the secretary's official "Journal of Congress." Once a session has been called to order, the wide double doors are closed; the only persons allowed to enter are delegates who can show proper credentials.

Doorman Andrew MacNair has his instructions, and the old man takes pride in the responsibilities he has been given as guard. He is meticulous about those credentials. No visitor, curious or otherwise, has ever gained admittance while Congress is in session.

This Monday morning, July first, has dawned clear and bright. At six A.M. the temperature reading is 68 degrees; a warm, soft breeze is blowing in from the south. Most of the delegates have been up since daybreak—reading, drafting statements, and completing last-minute correspondence in their furnished rooms across the city. Just last Thursday Congress advanced its meeting hour from ten to nine in the morning as a concession to the sometimes overpowering humidity of the hot summer weather. Now there seems to be even less time to complete the many tasks that must be finished before each morning session has begun.

Sentiment among the delegates is widely varied. There are those who are eagerly awaiting today's meeting; men whose expectations are high that, at last, the independence of the thirteen colonies will become a reality. There are others—doubtful, suspicious, uneasy about the future. Whatever their reactions, each is conscious that the vote he will probably be asked to cast today will have its effect in the New World for generations to come. It has not been an easy decision.

Over at Mrs. Yard's boarding house on Arch Street near the waterfront, John Adams is writing a hasty note to a friend in Georgia: "This morning is assigned to the greatest debate of all. A declaration that these colonies are free and independent states has been reported. . . . This day or tomorrow is to determine its fate."

Member of more committees than any other delegate, the stocky little lawyer from Massachusetts is undoubtedly the busiest man in Congress. In pursuing the cause of independence, he has closed his profitable law office in Boston and ended all private professional activity. His wife and children have been forced to eke out a small existence on the farm at Braintree, and now his beloved farm is in "enemy territory." There are many personal anxieties, yet he is giving everything to the cause to which he is dedicated.

To John Adams this promises to be a momentous day—the culmination, perhaps, of all he has worked for so incessantly. How well he remembers that morning three weeks ago—on June seventh—when Richard Henry Lee, head of the Virginia delegation, arose and presented his resolution on independence to Congress. Acting on instructions from the Sixth Virginia Convention, Lee proposed, "That these United Colonies are, and of right ought to be, free and independent States, that they are absolved from all allegiance to the British Crown, and that all political connection between them and the State of Great Britain is, and ought to be, totally dissolved."

His words electrified the assembled delegates. Without hesitation John Adams bounded to his feet to second the motion. But reaction, for the most part, was hostile to such "violent measures." Furious words ensued, some of the members even threatening to walk out should Mr. Lee's resolution be adopted. It was after seven o'clock when the day's session finally adjourned.

Debate continued throughout the following day, Saturday, and the intervening Sunday had done nothing to lessen the hot tempers of the delegates when they convened on Monday morning, June tenth. The members resolved themselves into a committee of the whole, a parliamentary device which they often found useful. For important decisions, the committee of the whole could take a "trial vote," which permitted a sampling of the prevailing sentiment without the binding necessity of recording the vote.

When the delegates had first met, more than two years ago, it had been agreed that they would operate under "the unit rule." Each colony would have one vote, a vote to be determined by polling the delegation present. If the representatives of any colony were deadlocked—say, two for and two against—that colony would be recorded as having no vote. No procedure had ever been defined for the election of delegates, nor had any specific number been assigned. Some were elected by their legislative assemblies;

other colonies held conventions to appoint their delegates. Originally Congress was, of course, an unofficial body, without any legal authority and, as yet, not recognized by any government in the world.

When the trial vote was taken on that Monday, June tenth, the majority still remained against adoption of the controversial resolution. There could be no compromise, no halfway measures. Divided though they were among themselves, there was still a strong sentiment that the outside world must see only a unified Congress.

Suddenly, Edward Rutledge of South Carolina jumped up and proposed that the decision on Mr. Lee's resolution be postponed for three weeks, until Monday, July first. There were many who would gladly have seen it postponed indefinitely.

Now the momentous Monday has arrived. The resolution which is to be taken up today is not something that Mr. Lee has proposed on impulse. Far from it. The first stirrings for independence began more than thirteen years ago, encouraged by the fact that the American colonists had actually enjoyed more liberty than many other subjects of the king.

For more than one hundred years, the colonies had been relatively independent. Even when there was a royal governor appointed by the Crown, each colony had been free to manage its own affairs to a high degree. Parliament had full authority to intervene in colonial affairs, but rarely did so. No new taxes were imposed. And for the most part, the colonists governed themselves. The experience of freedom became more and more ingrained.

The French and Indian War ended victoriously for
Great Britain in 1760. Canada was added to the British empire in North America, but the war had caused
a severe drain on the royal treasury. When George III
ascended the throne in 1760, he stubbornly insisted
that the colonies must help bear the brunt of the increased expenses.

At first the British customs officials were instructed
to clamp down on collecting the duty due under exist-
ing trade laws, which had long been evaded. Smug-
gling goods into the colonies had become a common
practice. It was hoped that a more rigid collection of
customs would increase revenues for the Crown.
Then, in 1763, Parliament began imposing heavy new
taxes. The Stamp Act first, then the Townshend Acts
brought bitter objection. The people reacted violently
to "taxation without representation." Eventually the
Crown backed down and in 1770 repealed all taxes except those on molasses and tea.

Nevertheless, even these taxes rankled the Massachusetts men who were leading the movement of resist-
ance. Late on the afternoon of December 16, 1773, a
group of Boston patriots donned Indian costumes,
stormed aboard three British ships lying in the harbor,
and threw 342 chests of tea overboard.

As punishment for "the Boston Tea Party," the British Parliament retaliated by setting up a military gov-

ernment in Massachusetts and closing the port of Boston to all trade. Instead of making the Bostonians feel guilty, as it was intended to do, the act provoked the patriots into organizing their own independent government. Sister colonies came to the rescue by sending in great wagonloads of grain, herds of cattle, money and supplies.

Opposition to Britain's new "tough" policy brought unity among the colonies, as nothing else had done thus far. There was a call for a meeting to consider "common grievances." And on September 5, 1774, delegates from every colony, with the exception of far-away Georgia, met in Philadelphia, determined to discover what was the best course to follow.

Rebellion was in the offing, but as yet the sentiment for independence had not fired men's minds. Indeed, George Washington wrote soon after Congress first met: "I think I can announce it as a fact that it is not the wish or interest of that government [Massachusetts] or any other upon this continent, separately or collectively, to set up for independence."

After some seven weeks, the Congress adjourned, resolving to meet the following spring if there had been no "redress of grievances" by George III and Parliament in answer to their petitions.

Even after the first shots were fired at Lexington and Concord in April 1775, there was still little inclination toward independence. The Second Continental Congress, convening the following month, voted to raise an army to resist British onslaughts but concluded their resolution by saying: "Lest this declaration should disquiet the minds of our friends and fellow-subjects in any part of the empire, we assure them that we mean not to dissolve that Union which has so long and so happily subsisted between us, and which we sincerely wish to see restored."

As the months passed, it became more and more evident that the British Crown had no intention of making any concessions to "the wicked rebels" in America. The idea of separating from the mother country was being agitated primarily by the New England delegations. Yet many were reluctant to challenge the might of the British Empire. There was much talk of reconciliation.

In January 1776, the publication of the pamphlet *Common Sense*, written by Thomas Paine, began attracting attention throughout the colonies. Worded in simple but powerful language, the treatise attacked the British monarchy as an institution. Paine praised the virtues of a republic, arguing that independence was merely "the common sense of the matter" and that "a government of our own is a natural right." At the same time George III declared the colonies to be in a state of rebellion.

Now the movement for independence began gathering force. A defiant Congress organized a navy, armed privately owned merchant vessels, prohibited trade with Britain, and opened American ports to the rest of the world. In an even bolder gesture, they sent the Connecticut delegate Silas Deane to France, to seek assistance from a country still traditionally hostile to England.

Among the Congressional delegates, there were a number who had been instructed by their colonial assemblies to refrain from voting for independence. Others felt they should not commit themselves without approval from the governing body back home. However, the men agitating for independence have continued to work ardently, holding political conclaves in their rooms during the evening hours, putting forth their most persuasive arguments.

As the momentum increased, John Adams had good cause to write: "Every day rolls in upon us Independence like a torrent." Virginia, oldest of the Colonies, had made the fatal determination on May fifteenth. It was their instructions that prompted Richard Henry Lee to make his memorable proposal on June seventh.

By now everyone knows that New England is solidly backing the move for independence. The South is firmer than anyone could have hoped for—only South Carolina is wavering. It is the Middle Colonies that give cause for grave concern.

The New York Assembly is not anxious to sever ties

with Great Britain; most of its members are loyal Tories. However, the New York delegates attending the sessions in Philadelphia have been caught up in the wave of sentiment for independence. They have written urgent letters asking to have their instructions changed.

Pennsylvania, richest and most powerful of all the colonies, poses a serious problem. Just two weeks ago the Assembly voted to remove the anti-independence instructions. Delegates are now free to vote according to their own consciences, but among the seven delegates, only old Dr. Franklin favors the idea. As long as a majority balks at breaking ties with Great Britain, there's little chance that the resolution can be passed with unanimity.

The members from Delaware are divided among themselves. The Maryland delegates favor independence, but their instructions have been to vote against it. On June nineteenth a letter from the New Jersey Assembly informed Congress that their royal governor had been removed from office. The pro-independence men have taken over the colony's business, and the delegates opposed to independence have been recalled. Five new representatives, all enthusiastic patriots, are presumably on their way to Philadelphia at this very moment.

Certainly now it can only be a question of time.

To John Adams these past three weeks have seemed interminable. The maneuvering after each day's session, the shuffling and shifting of names on lists in order to be sure there would be sufficient votes for the Lee resolution—all this has taken much of his time. Adams' constituents back in Massachusetts have only added to the confusion with letters asking just what Congress is doing, "Is it dozing, amusing itself?" He has answered by writing, "Remember, you can't make thirteen Clocks strike precisely alike, at the same Second."

Yet John Adams has to admit to himself that politically the three-week waiting period has been a wise move. If the vote had been taken on June seventh, those favoring independence would surely have lost. It's encouraging to know that the leader of the Maryland delegation, Samuel Chase (sometimes called "Bacon-Face" because of his ruddy complexion), has been back in his own colony for more than two weeks now. He's been riding through the countryside, canvassing his constituents, trying to persuade the Assembly in Annapolis that the colony is thoroughly independence-minded. He wants the anti-independence instructions to the Maryland delegates removed.

There may be some word from Chase today. In any case, a stiff fight lies ahead in Congress this morning —of this, John Adams is confident. And as the most articulate spokesman for the patriots, he knows he'll probably bear the brunt of that fight.

Across the hall in Mrs. Yard's boarding house, the oldest delegate from Massachusetts is also making final preparations for today's meeting, the long-awaited session which may bring the fulfillment of his hopes.

For the past twenty years Samuel Adams has worked for only one cause: independence. Notoriously indifferent to business and financial affairs, Adams is a skilled politician, astute, persuasive. No one has done more in behalf of American liberty. Reticent in public, he works most effectively behind the scenes. It is Sam Adams who originated the underground "Committees of Correspondence" four years ago, an organization designed to keep the revolutionary groups in Massachusetts closely in touch with each other, an idea that has now spread to all the colonies. As an active participant, he has written thousands of letters, hoping to plant the seeds of revolution in men's minds. And he was one of the leaders of the notorious Boston Tea Party, an act that put a price on his head.

This morning Sam Adams has dressed with more care than usual, putting on the dark-red broadcloth suit and the short black cape that several anonymous well-wishers in Boston have provided for the usually shabbily dressed patriot. With cocked hat in hand, he opens the door and goes to knock on his cousin John's door.

It will only be a minute, John Adams calls, as he stuffs a sheaf of papers into a small green satchel, the cloth case he has carried since first he took up the study of law. Conscious of the value of a neat appearance, he pauses before the brass wall sconce to adjust his wig, patting the little powdered rolls into place over his ears.

★★ 2 ★★

FRED GRAFF'S TENANT

Just a few blocks away, the lodger in Mr. Frederick Graff's brick dwelling has been up since five. The sandy-haired lawyer from Virginia is well pleased with his accommodations. The house is new, just completed by bricklayer Graff, and situated at the corner of Seventh and Market Streets in a neighborhood where, as yet, there are few other houses. The new tenant moved in little more than a month ago from lodgings at Benjamin Randall's, because he wanted the benefit of "a freely circulating air." Since Mr. Jefferson can't be at his beloved Monticello, this seems the most acceptable answer—a large bedroom and spacious parlor, separated by a hallway.

Thirty-three-year-old Thomas Jefferson is a man

well over six feet tall, slim and erect. His ruddy face is
freckled from long years of riding through the Virginia countryside. One observer has described him as
looking "much like a tall large-boned farmer." Having
studied law for five years at the College of William
and Mary, Jefferson thought he wanted to practice
professionally. But just two years ago he decided to
devote all his time to public affairs. He's been an active member of the Virginia House of Burgesses,
standing firmly behind his friend Patrick Henry in
championing the colonists' rights.

Last year he was elected as a delegate to the Second
Continental Congress. He replaced Peyton Randolph
who had died in October, having served as the first
president of the Continental Congress. Mr. Jefferson's
reputation as a writer preceded him to Philadelphia;
he was soon given a number of papers to draft for
Congress. Modest and courteous, the Virginia delegate has a gentle manner that has impressed his colleagues, yet he is reticent about his personal affairs.
The sometimes caustic John Adams wrote of him,
"Though a silent member of the Congress, he was so
prompt, frank, explicit and decisive upon committee
and in conversation . . . that he soon seized upon my
heart."

This morning Mr. Jefferson has dressed quickly,
knowing there is much to accomplish before nine

o'clock. He walks across the hall and goes immediately to his living-room work table. Taking down the portable writing box which Cabinetmaker Randall built to his design, he unfolds the hinged top, opens the drawer below, and pulls out paper, a quill pen, and tiny hand-blown inkwell, in order to complete a number of committee reports. That drawer, too, makes a fine repository for the new thermometer he has just purchased. The box is not only convenient to carry back and forth to sessions at the State House, but it has been advantageous for the work he has done here in his lodgings.

These past three weeks have indeed been hectic. Constant committee meetings—reports to prepare, some of them lengthy. And he was also assigned the task of drawing up the rough draft for a declaration of independence.

After the postponement of Mr. Lee's resolution on June tenth, Congress decided that some sort of declaration should be ready—in case the resolution is voted in the affirmative—and a Committee of Five was assigned to the task: Thomas Jefferson, John Adams, Benjamin Franklin, Roger Sherman, and Robert R. Livingston.

Benjamin Franklin was too busy to try the writing. Sherman and Livingston are less adept with words; thus the task of drafting fell on John Adams and

Thomas Jefferson. Years later, Adams would report that the following conversation then ensued over the authorship:

ADAMS: "I said I will not: You shall do it."

JEFFERSON: "Oh no! Why will you not? You ought to do it."

ADAMS: "I will not."

JEFFERSON: "Why?"

ADAMS: "Reasons enough."

JEFFERSON: "What can be your reasons?"

ADAMS: "Reason 1st. You are a Virginian and Virginia ought to appear at the head of this business. Reason 2nd, I am obnoxious, suspected, and unpopular; You are very much otherwise. Reason 3d, You can write ten times better than I can."

JEFFERSON: "Well, if you are decided, I will do as well as I can."

Night after night the Virginian sat in his parlor with his writing box propped on his knees, his quill pen moving swiftly across the paper as his mind raced far ahead of his fingers. Sometimes he would stop to reread a sentence. Not satisfied, he would draw a line through several words, penning in the change above.

First there is the preamble, a dignified and forthright statement of intention. Next comes a lengthy second paragraph, setting forth the philosophical reasons for the break with England. In this paragraph, Jefferson has drawn on his life-long study of philosophy and his familiarity with the Englishman John Locke and Locke's treatises on the basic rights of man. It is also probable that Jefferson was influenced by the "Declaration of Rights," penned by his friend George Mason for the colony of Virginia and published in the *Pennsylvania Evening Post* last June sixth. Mason wrote:

> That all men are born equally free and independant and have certain inherent natural Rights, of which they can not, by any Compact, deprive or divest their Posterity; among which are the Enjoyment of Life and Liberty, with the Means of Acquiring and possessing property, and pursuing and obtaining Happiness and Safety.

Thomas Jefferson has taken this idea and translated it into more positive terms. Underscoring equality as the basis of natural rights, he has written:

> We hold these truths to be sacred & undeniable that all men are created equal & independant, that from that equal creation they derive rights inherent & inalienable, among which are the preservation of life, & liberty & the pursuit of happiness.

The third part of the Declaration, and by far the longest, is the list of charges against George III. These are not indictments hastily thought up in a few days' time. They are real and specific grievances which Thomas Jefferson has heard stated and restated for many months in order to justify the colonies' position. The final paragraphs contain the formal statement of the colonies' intention—to sever all ties with England and declare themselves free and independent states.

In composing the Declaration, Thomas Jefferson has sought to put into words the justice of America's desire for independence. If Congress should adopt this paper, it would then become the official statement of the thirteen new states. He must, therefore, present America's case to the world in terms that are crystal-clear, in words that no man can fail to understand.

Once finished, Jefferson took his writing to Mr. Adams. Everything considered, the Massachusetts man gave hearty approval to Jefferson's document, although he does think that calling King George a "tyrant" is a little harsh. Perhaps that term should be stricken. Later John Adams would write: "I was delighted with its high tone and the flights of oratory with which it abounded."

The young author then called on Dr. Franklin. Troubled by gout, the old Philadelphian greeted his guest from an armchair, his feet resting on a footstool. With keen interest Benjamin Franklin examined the document, making only a few minor changes. Possibly,

it was he who suggested that instead of "We hold
these truths to be sacred and undeniable," the wording should be "We hold these truths to be self-evi-

dent . . . ," a change that the young man interlined
on his rough draft. On the whole, Dr. Franklin was
delighted with what Thomas Jefferson has written—
and told him so.

The fourth member of the committee, the "solid
and sensible" Roger Sherman, also added his approval.
He read the draft slowly, nodding with pleasure as he
went over the sentences, which reflect so well what he
himself felt but could never have put so eloquently.
Roger Sherman had no changes to suggest; he was,
indeed, pleased with Mr. Jefferson's writing.

The fifth committee member, Robert Livingston,
was not consulted; he had returned to his home in
New York. Grave doubts had developed in Livingston's mind about the wisdom of declaring independence—it is too audacious a step. He has, therefore,
taken the easy way out by resigning his position as a
delegate.

After consulting with his colleagues, Mr. Jefferson
took the much interlined paper and recopied it. Just
last Friday, June 28, he placed the fresh copy—"the
fair copy" as it is called—on Secretary Thomson's
desk. With this document Jefferson has sought to
shape a new pattern of thought for America. According to custom, the Secretary read it to the members;
then it was "ordered to lie on the table" until Monday.

Now the long-awaited day has arrived, the day that means so much to the men who have been agitating for independence. If Congress approves Mr. Lee's resolution, the paper drafted by Mr. Jefferson is ready for approval. But first, the Middle Colonies must abandon their conservative leanings. If only they will join the patriots' cause . . .

Thomas Jefferson's reports are finished. He folds up his writing box and steps to the window, throwing open the wide double casement. A refreshing breeze— yes, but it seems tinged with warmth. There may be some rain before nightfall. For a moment he stands fascinated by the ribbon of river to the southeast— the winding blue Delaware filled with sloops and schooners whose sails are silhouetted against the Jersey shoreline. There are always ships to watch, if one has the time. The port of Philadelphia is the busiest in the colonies, with sailing vessels bringing in cargo from all over the world—spices from Java, silk and sugar from India, cork and olives from Spain, pepper from Sumatra.

The Virginia delegate heaves a sigh. If Congress adopts Mr. Lee's resolution, there will certainly be debate on the declaration he has prepared. All those hours of arduous work at his desk . . . it's going to be hard to hear his writing torn apart. A glance at the clock shows that it's now eight thirty—time to set out for the State House, come what may.

★★ 3 ★★

THE HOUR OF NINE
APPROACHES

As the hot July sun rises higher, traffic increases along the broad tree-lined streets in this, the largest city in America. Heavy wagons rumble over the cobblestones, carrying farm produce to Philadelphia's water-front market stalls. There's a clatter of shiny carriages as men ride to their downtown offices.

Merchants and clerks are hurrying to their counting-houses. Leather-aproned apprentices bring their wheel-barrows to a halt as they pause at the public water pumps to watch the servant girls drawing water. Small boys playing pitch-penny idle along the brick foot-ways, while artisans and mechanics en route to work thread their way through the games.

With matters unsettled at the State House, there is

little more than rumor to go on. For the carpenters
and tailors, the bricklayers and weavers, the printers,
coopers, and clockmakers, their daily tasks must still
be pursued. Let the politicians take care of colonial
affairs.

The hands of the great clock on the State House
tower show that the Congressional delegates will soon
be arriving for the day's deliberations. David Ritten-
house, Philadelphia's eminent astronomer, ambles
down the front steps of the building at Fifth and
Chestnut. He has just finished the first of his twice-
daily inspections of the clock's mechanism, a self-
appointed task, but one he considers a privilege since

most of the city's thirty thousand inhabitants regulate
their lives by this timepiece.

Everything is in readiness for today's session in the
red-brick State House. When the Continental Congress first convened, its members met in Carpenter's
Hall, two blocks down the street. But last year the
Pennsylvania Assembly graciously offered the delegates the use of their first-floor chamber in the State
House, moving across the hall into the Pennsylvania
Supreme Court's room for their own intermittent
gatherings.

The most impressive building in all Philadelphia,

the State House is Georgian in design. When the Pennsylvania Assembly decided to erect the building, back in 1732, the entire square between Fifth and Sixth Streets was purchased to give the new building "a worthy setting." It was decided that the State House should front on Chestnut Street, leaving a large yard behind it, bounded by Walnut Street on the south.

On the main floor are two large high-ceilinged rooms, separated by a wide lobby, the room on the east side being the one the Continental Congress is occupying. All the delegates enter the building through the single massively carved doorway that opens onto Chestnut Street. Above the door hangs the royal coat of arms, symbol of his Majesty's authority in America.

The meeting room is a white-paneled chamber, much more spacious than the delegates' former quarters in Carpenter's Hall. From the center of the ceiling hangs a handsome crystal chandelier. On the wall opposite the doorway are brass-fitted twin fireplaces; between them a low dais has been erected for the president's table and chair. The table is fitted with a massive silver inkwell, and just to the right is the mace, a tall silver staff—the presidential insignia of authority. The president's chair has a delicately carved high back, at the top of which is painted a rising sun.

The arms and seat are leather-padded, edged with ornamental brass nails.

On the broad west wall at the back of the room is a decorative panoply—a drum, swords, and banner captured last year at Fort Ticonderoga by Ethan Allen and Benedict Arnold. Allen, in collecting the trophies, shouted that he was taking the place, "In the name of the Great Jehovah and the Continental Congress."

The comfortable padded chairs for the delegates are a vast improvement over the wooden-bottomed Windsor chairs at Carpenter's Hall. There's more table space, too—where members may spread out their papers, take notes, or write letters, if the session becomes boresome. However, everyone knows that today's meeting will be taut with controversy. There will be no time for dillydallying.

Tall windows line two sides of the room, windows that might admit plenty of air if it were possible to have them wide open while Congress is sitting. But the business of Congress is much too important to chance the possibility of being overheard by passersby; therefore, the windows are opened only a crack from the top, the theory being that this will allow some slight passage of air for ventilation. In reality, the opening serves instead as a fine passageway for horseflies from the livery stable across the street. Many a moving speech has been punctuated by loud slaps as the insects prey upon the delegates' silk-stockinged legs.

The men who will meet here this morning are still sharply divided on the issue at stake. Those who want to declare independence immediately—the New Englanders and the Virginians—are called "the violent men." But the majority of delegates are still urging that a more moderate course be pursued, that some compromise can surely be worked out with the British. This group has become known as "the cool considerate men," the conservatives.

Five miles north of Philadelphia at his luxurious country estate, Fairhill, John Dickinson, the Quaker lawyer, is in his library, assembling notes for the speech he intends to give at this morning's session. As the leader of the moderates, Dickinson is ready to break with the radical men. True enough, the author of *Letters from a Farmer in Pennsylvania*—a book for which he has become justly famous—has steadily championed the cause of colonial rights. But he has always emphasized that change should be gradual, that any dispute must be resolved by patient reasoning rather than by violence.

At first Dickinson had wide support among the members of the Second Continental Congress. During the past few months, however, his leadership has been challenged by the obviously growing strength of "the violent men." He is well aware that this morning's speech may be the most important of his life.

Pale and taut, the lawyer bids farewell to his wife, Mary, and climbs into his carriage for the drive into Philadelphia. Mary has never been interested in politics, a fact her husband finds hard to understand since her late father, Isaac Norris, was the speaker of the Pennsylvania Assembly. It was Norris who ordered the great bell which hangs in the State House steeple. And it was he who chose the inscription which is engraved on the rim of the bell: "Proclaim liberty throughout the land, unto all the inhabitants thereof." There is a rumor that once the resolution on independence is adopted the great bell will be rung. John Dickinson cannot help but hope that this will never happen.

Over at Daniel Smyth's City Tavern—the smartest lodging place in town—the youngest member of Congress, twenty-six-year-old Edward Rutledge, is making last-minute preparations for today's session. Adjusting his brightly colored silk knee breeches and satin waistcoat, he preens for a few moments before the full-length mirror, though he knows that his fellow delegates—Middleton, Lynch, and Heyward—are impatiently waiting in the dining room downstairs.

John Adams has confided to his diary that this young leader of the South Carolina delegation is "a perfect Bob-o-Lincoln . . . a peacock. Excessively vain, excessively weak." Though vanity may be one of his faults, Ned Rutledge is anything but weak; he is a very determined young man with ideas that do not always agree with those of "the violent men." He has called Mr. Lee's resolution "a blind precipitous measure" and has been vociferously opposed to it since the day it was proposed. In his view, the New Englanders are to blame for the present state of affairs, and if they are allowed to continue on this dangerous course, it can bring nothing to the colonies but calamity.

Rutledge and his three fellow delegates are all members of wealthy South Carolina plantation families. All four are lawyers, having studied at the Middle Temple in London. They are strong "local patriots," with a dread of giving too much authority to a central governing body like the Continental Congress. They realize that today's session is bound to be a battle.

In front of the Widow Graydon's slate-roofed mansion, the president of the Congress, John Hancock of Massachusetts, is climbing into his handsome coach with its liveried driver. One of the wealthiest men in America, Hancock has rented the mansion for his young wife, the former Dolly Quincy of Braintree, during their stay in Philadelphia. On this day, above all days, he intends to be punctual for the meeting at the State House.

Nearly six feet tall, John Hancock looks the part of an aristocrat, from his smartly dressed wig to his grained-leather pumps. At times he seems vain, arrogant—he's even been dubbed "King Hancock." But he's every inch a patriot, with a passionate hatred of injustice. Long active in Massachusetts politics, Hancock joined Sam Adams in leading the raid on those tea-laden ships in Boston Harbor three years ago. Much of his wealth comes from Boston property, but when General Washington was considering the possibility of setting a torch to Boston, Hancock, without a moment's hesitation, urged him to do so.

Though not a handsome man—his finely chiseled nose is too thin, his upper jaw too heavy for the rest of his face—John Hancock has a kind of personal magnetism. There are many who deplore his pretentious mannerisms, but no one has ever criticized the way he conducts the business of the Continental Congress. As he drives along Chestnut Street this morning, Hancock passes Dr. Franklin who is being carried in a sedan chair by two husky parolees from the City Jail on Walnut Street.

At the age of seventy Benjamin Franklin is so crippled by gout that he finds the easiest way to get about is to ride in a sedan chair. A short stout man in plain

Quaker dress, Dr. Franklin is undoubtedly the best-known citizen of Philadelphia, possibly the best-known in America. When he first came to the city, more than fifty years ago, as a runaway printer's devil from Boston, Franklin possessed only a single Dutch dollar. Philadelphia was much smaller then—with a population of some ten thousand people.

This morning as he rides through the broad streets in his bobbing sedan chair, the old gentleman smiles with pleasure. Philadelphia is his city and he loves it dearly; he has spent much time and effort in its improvement. The street lamps and the public water pumps on nearly every corner, the lightning rods on the rooftops, the public library, the hospital, the municipal fire department—these and much more bear witness to the inventive mind of Benjamin Franklin.

But what of this Monday morning? How will the delegates react to the bold proposal slated for discussion? Franklin knows that among his own Pennsylvania delegation there is a strong conservative feeling, that he alone favors independence. John Morton? He seems to be wavering, but the others—John Dickinson, Robert Morris, Charles Humphreys, and Thomas Willing—are avowed opponents of such a drastic move.

The sedan chair has come to a stop in front of the

main entrance to the State House. As he climbs down Dr. Franklin catches sight of his gathering colleagues. Heavy-set Benjamin Harrison, from Virginia, is talking heatedly with a fellow delegate, tobacco merchant Carter Braxton. John Adams and his cousin Samuel are huddled with peppery little Elbridge Gerry from Massachusetts and the ex-shoemaker from Connecticut, Roger Sherman.

Now the delegates are mounting the three steps and walking through the wide doorway on Chestnut Street. The hall seems cool after the heat outdoors; the dark plank floor, a grateful contrast to the shining cobblestone streets.

At the far end of the hallway, the door leading outside is open, revealing the sycamore trees now in full leaf. The yard itself resembles a pasture, its uneven ground covered by unkempt grass, wild shrubs, and occasional huckleberry bushes. Nothing has been yet done to beautify it. Just six years ago the Pennsylvania Assembly ordered the yard enclosed by a seven-foot brick wall, thus insuring some measure of privacy for those wanting to stroll through its open spaces.

Bustling through the Chestnut Street door, John Adams pauses to give instructions to the doorman, Andy MacNair. If the Maryland post should arrive during this morning's session, please bring any letters to him—or to President Hancock—without delay.

The white-paneled meeting room is filling rapidly. Dr. Franklin is already seated in his favorite chair on the back row to the right. Next to him is Thomas Jefferson. The Virginian likes this place next to the windows which overlook the State House yard. He is not one given to entering the debate, and this is an excellent vantage point for silent observation. Now he places his writing box across his knees and unfolds the double-hinged lid. The desk top is ready, should he want to make any notes. At five minutes before nine, Jefferson methodically records the temperature shown on his new thermometer. It is 81.5 degrees, though the oppressive humidity makes it seem far warmer.

John Adams hustles into his place on the opposite side of the room, stowing away the ever-present green satchel on the window sill beside him. He notes that John Dickinson, James Wilson, and Edward Rutledge seem to be having an earnest conversation in the center of the room. Glancing about, Adams realizes that several of the pro-independence men are missing. Caesar Rodney is in Delaware, and Samuel Chase has not yet returned from Annapolis. It's going to be precarious—this adoption of Mr. Lee's resolution—if it succeeds at all. The struggle will be a bitter one— no doubt about that.

President Hancock has already taken his seat behind the large table on the dais facing the delegates. At a desk placed a little to the left is Charles Thomson, secretary of the Congress, sometimes known as "the Samuel Adams of Philadelphia" because of his radical views. He is a thin little man with piercing eyes; his hair is his own, and he wears it unfashionably short above his ears. Now he shuffles the papers and jots down reminders for the day's session. Thomson has no vote in the proceedings, although he considers it a great honor to have been chosen as secretary. His minutes in the Journal of Congress are as meticulous as they are discreet; he is well aware that he must never record a lost motion or the details of a debate.

The quiet hum of conversation continues, a medley of voices interspersed with drawling Southern accents and an occasional Yankee twang. More than half the delegates are lawyers, many having studied in England. A number are successful merchants and plantation owners. They are all responsible men, chosen as delegates because of their respect for law and order. There is no thought of conspiracy or fly-by-night rebellion. And less than a year ago there was no hint of breaking away from the mother country. The hope of reconciliation is uppermost in many of the delegates' minds—despite the resolution which they know is to come up for debate today.

The clock in the tower strikes nine, and a sober silence engulfs the meeting room. . . .

★★ 4 ★★

THE DAY'S SESSION

John Hancock brings down his gavel with an authoritative rap. As president of Congress, he thoroughly enjoys the small ceremonies of that office. Nodding to Secretary Thomson, the president reaches for the set of papers that he is to read to the assembled delegates.

Despite the pressing nature of the resolution on independence, the normal business of Congress must first be transacted. There are reports from General Washington and from Benedict Arnold, communications from the legislative assemblies, letters from commanders in the field. How to obtain supplies for the Continental army is an ever-pressing problem.

The members of Congress listen attentively, now

and then making suggestions. Occasionally one of them brings up an objection, which leads to a short-lived debate. All this is merely routine, however—it's been going on for almost a year. Secretary Thomson makes a terse entry in the Journal of Congress: "Sundry letters were laid before Congress and read. . . ."

As the morning drags on, the heat becomes more oppressive. The room is stuffy, and the bulbous horse-flies buzz around angrily, seeking out their prey. Outside, the low-hanging clouds swirl about the sky in ominous silence.

The delegates are becoming impatient with the continued reading of routine communications—an endless number, it seems. They twist in their chairs, clear their throats, whisper among themselves.

It is almost one o'clock before President Hancock announces that Congress will "resolve itself into a Committee of the Whole to take into consideration the resolution concerning independence." With his love of ceremony, the president reaches for the silver mace and hands it to Secretary Thomson. Now that the formal Congress has been dissolved, the members acting as a committee of the whole are free to express themselves without the necessity of their remarks being recorded officially.

John Hancock steps down from the dais and takes a seat among the Massachusetts delegates as Benjamin

Harrison, chairman of the committee of the whole, moves toward the vacant chair. He lets his huge bulk down gingerly, almost as if he were stuffing himself into the seat.

John Dickinson is on his feet at once. As the leader of the forces advocating moderation, he is spokesman for the fight against Lee's resolution. In an earnest voice he begins: "The consequences involved in the Motion now lying before you are of such magnitude that I tremble under the oppressive honor of sharing in its determination. . . . My conduct, this day, I expect will give the finishing blow to my once too great, and now too diminished, popularity. It will be my lot to know, that I had rather vote away the enjoyment of that dazzling display, than the blood and happiness of my countrymen."

The note of fervor in Dickinson's voice holds the members' careful attention. There can be little doubt of the man's sincerity. "I must speak, though I should lose my life, though I should lose the affections of my country."

There is a pause as the speaker bows his head in silent prayer for a moment. Then he reaches into his pocket and draws out the set of notes he has prepared for this, the most important speech of his career. "Gentlemen of very distinguished abilities and knowledge differ widely in their sentiments upon the point now agitated," he proclaims. "They all agree, that the utmost prudence is required in forming our decision, but immediately disagree in their notion of that prudence. . . ."

Seated in the front row, John Adams watches his adversary in stony silence, fearful that Dickinson's eloquence may win over those delegates yet undecided. But this is a gamble that "the violent men" must take.

As the speaker continues, the assembly chamber grows rapidly darker. The summer storm that has been brewing since midmorning is threatening to break at any moment. Jagged spurts of lightning are punctuated by thunder, rumbling in across the Delaware River.

At the back of the room the door opens, and Andy MacNair walks quietly up the side aisle to hand Mr. Hancock an official-looking envelope. Then he tiptoes toward the front row with a similar message for John Adams. Opening it, Mr. Adams reads, "I am this Moment from the House with a Unanimous Vote of our Convention for Independence . . . Your friend, S. Chase." Glancing back toward Hancock, Adams watches the president hold up his envelope and silently form the word "Maryland."

The quiet byplay has been observed by several of the delegates. As Dickinson continues speaking, there are whispers all over the room that "Maryland votes for independence."

"I say let us wait!" Dickinson raises his voice to compete with the gusty sheets of rain now beating against the windows. "Let us know if we can get terms from France that will be more beneficial. If we can, let us declare independence. If we cannot, let us at least withhold that declaration, till we obtain terms that are tolerable." He reminds Congress that three months ago Silas Deane of Connecticut was sent to Paris to try to persuade France to send munitions to the colonists and as yet there has been no word from him.

Though it is now not quite four o'clock, the room has grown very dark. Secretary Thomson hurries out to consult with the doorkeeper and very shortly a pair of large candelabra are placed on the president's table. The shadowy candlelight reveals that some of the delegates are still listening intently to Mr. Dickinson. Others have become bored; a few are even dozing. A thunderclap rattles the windows. No need to be frightened though; the knowledge of Dr. Franklin's lightning rods mounted atop the State House brings reassurance. Even though a bolt of lightning should strike the tower, the rod would carry it safely toward the ground.

Mr. Dickinson is still speaking, repeating the old

arguments against independence in a voice that has become more and more insistent. John Adams continues to watch the faces around him, weighing the chances for unanimity.

Maryland is a sure victory, now that the note has arrived from Samuel Chase. But what about New Jersey? The delegates who favor independence are supposedly on their way—but why haven't they arrived? Delaware is divided, as everyone is well aware. Colonel McKean is a firm independence man, but George Read remains opposed. Caesar Rodney would vote "Aye," but he is in Delaware on militia business. New York is still waiting for new instructions. South Carolina has announced no decision. And how can the delegation from Pennsylvania possibly be won over?

While the speaker lists the dangers that lie ahead should the colonies pursue their rash act, Thomas McKean of Delaware gets up and walks toward the door at the back of the room. His unobtrusive exit is not lost on John Adams, however. Although delegates wander in and out during sessions, no one has stirred from his seat today. Perhaps Colonel McKean has something in mind. Mr. Adams wonders.

The strain of his lengthy speech is beginning to show in Dickinson's pale thin face. With his disavowal of what he considers the radicals' position, he has eliminated any chance of personal advancement, should a

new government actually be formed. Yet he is willing to take that risk as he utters his climactic close: "When our enemies are pressing us so vigorously, when we are in so wretched a state of preparation, when the sentiments and designs of our expected friends are so unknown to us, I am alarmed at this declaration being so vehemently presented. . . . I should be glad to read a little more in the Doomsday Book of America."

The speech is finished, but Dickinson stands for a moment, gazing at his compatriots. He has risked everything for this hour. Will they decide that moderation is the course to follow, after all? As the speaker takes his seat, the room is filled with an uncanny stillness. The delegates glance at each other uneasily.

There must be a rebuttal—someone must answer Dickinson. But who? Neither Benjamin Franklin nor Thomas Jefferson has ever uttered a word on the floor. Samuel Adams is too upset at the moment, and Roger Sherman doesn't feel competent. All eyes turn to John Adams.

But the burly little lawyer from Massachusetts does not rise immediately. He knows that his blunt delivery is no match for Dickinson's flights of oratory. The issues are clear enough. Yet he cannot allow the opposition to have the last word.

Slowly John Adams gets to his feet, assuming his

characteristic stance—legs wide apart, arms behind his back, his right hand clasping his left wrist. Later he will write his wife, Abby, that at this moment he wished for "the talents and eloquence of the ancient orators of Greece and Rome." Though his words are not recorded, his speech receives high praise from his colleagues. Jefferson, years later, will note that John Adams was "our Colossus on the floor . . . not graceful nor eloquent, not remarkably fluent, but he came out occasionally with a power of thought and expression, that moved us from our seats."

The fury of the storm outside begins to abate as Adams describes the successive steps of the crisis with Britain, the efforts at reconciliation, and the advantages that are to be gained by declaring independence at once. Before he has finished, the door at the back of the room is flung open.

Five rain-spattered men enter, still booted and spurred, and wait in silence until Mr. Adams takes his seat. Then the newcomers come forward to present their credentials to Chairman Harrison. They are the recently elected delegates from New Jersey: the Reverend John Witherspoon, Judge Richard Stockton, Francis Hopkinson, John Hart, and Abraham Clark. They apologize for their tardy appearance, explaining that the rain has delayed them.

As spokesman for the group, the Reverend Mr.

Witherspoon asks to hear a review of the arguments. John Adams does not stir. But the clergyman is not to be put off. He repeats the request, this time more insistently.

Edward Rutledge steps over to John Adams. "Nobody will speak but you on this subject," he says. "You have all the topics so ready, that you must satisfy the gentlemen from New Jersey."

Adams protests that he is not an actor or gladiator to be exhibited "for the entertainment of the audience," that he would be embarrassed to repeat what he has said at least "twenty times before," that he has nothing new to add.

As Rutledge continues his prodding, John Adams once more rises wearily. He knows that the delegates from New Jersey have already been instructed to vote for independence. Still, as individuals, they are privileged to change their minds. Despite the fact that Adams feels it "an idle misspense of time," he recapitulates the argument for independence.

Brief though his remarks are, John Adams has the talent for making the future seem something worth fighting for. When Richard Stockton returns to New Jersey, he will tell his friends that "the Man to whom the Country is most indebted for the great measure of Independence is Mr. John Adams of Boston—I call him the Atlas of American Independence."

After Adams has finished, there is further wrangling among the delegates. Two more speeches are made by the forces opposed to independence. Can this dissension ever be resolved? Will they ever reach unanimity?

Roger Sherman addresses the chair, asking that a trial vote be taken in committee of the whole. Chairman Harrison calls for order, nodding to Secretary Thomson to begin the roll call.

"New Hampshire . . . Massachusetts . . . Rhode Island . . . Connecticut . . ."

The secretary's voice continues through all thirteen colonies until he hears Button Gwinnett's "Aye" for Georgia. The final tabulation shows nine colonies for independence, four against. Pennsylvania and South Carolina have answered with a vehement "Nay." New York has abstained from voting, "for want of instructions from home." And Delaware is divided—Thomas McKean is for it, and George Read against it. Only Caesar Rodney can swing Delaware's vote to independence.

Edward Rutledge springs to his feet, requesting that the final decision be postponed until tomorrow. There is a possibility, he implies, that South Carolina may change its mind.

The committee of the whole is dissolved, and President Hancock resumes his chair on the dais, replacing

the silver mace. Benjamin Harrison formally reports
that the committee of the whole has asked "leave to sit
again" and that the final decision will be made tomorrow.

There is further business—two more letters to be
read. But now the delegates are weary, after a session
that has lasted for more than nine hours. The letters
are quickly referred to the Board of War.

President Hancock raps his gavel, and the Congress
is adjourned until nine o'clock tomorrow morning.

★★ 5 ★★

AFTER THE MEETING ADJOURNS

The delegates arise with relief. From his back-row seat, Mr. Jefferson is among the first to slip away after President Hancock dismisses Congress. A man of few words, he never stops to exchange pleasantries with his colleagues. Now he strides east along Chestnut Street, peering curiously at the long, low wooden shed adjacent to the State House.

The chiefs of the Six Nations have been housed here for the past several weeks. They have come to Philadelphia for "council-fires" on the invitation of Congress, the hope being that the Indians will be persuaded to remain neutral in the conflict with Great Britain. In fact, it was on June eleventh that the chiefs were last called to the meeting room at the State House.

President Hancock made an appropriate speech, hoping that "the friendship which is between us and you will be firm and continue as long as the sun shall shine and the waters run . . ." The ceremony was concluded with presents for the Indians.

Now, striding past the shed, Thomas Jefferson recalls how pleased the red men seemed by the occasion, how Chief White-Eyes, as spokesman, christened President Hancock with the name "K-ran-du-awn," or "Great-Tree-of-Liberty." It was an amicable afternoon, duly noted in the official Journal.

Lately, however, the presence of the Indians has been forgotten under the mounting pressure of the independence question. They have been left to themselves, though Mr. Jefferson has heard the doorkeeper complain that they are careless with fire. And this wooden shed is highly inflammable.

At the State House the white-paneled meeting chamber is being rapidly emptied of Congressmen. The delegates are anxious to escape the oppressive humidity, which has enveloped the room as an aftermath of the afternoon storm. Fortunately the rain has stopped, though a still-threatening sky suggests this may be merely a lull in the violent weather.

Only John Adams remains seated, lost for a few moments in private speculation. Silently he is shuffling and reshuffling the names of the delegates. Independence is far from a certainty. The new instructions from the Maryland Assembly are encouraging, but South Carolina has just voted "Nay." Still it was that young popinjay Rutledge who asked for postponement. Could this possibly mean that he is working on the South Carolina men to change their vote—or is he just trying to stall?

Delaware continues to be an enigma. Colonel McKean advocates independence, but George Read can't be budged from his opposition. Since Caesar Rodney is absent, Delaware's vote is canceled. And the prospect of winning over a majority of the Pennsylvania delegation continues to seem unlikely.

More than any other delegate to Congress, John Adams realizes that the colonies must be unanimous in their final vote, or there will be a dangerous split in the new nation. Any dissenting colony might become a beachhead for the invading British. This must not be allowed to happen. There's work to be done tonight behind the scenes; the opposition must be persuaded. Adams reaches for his green cloth satchel and hurries toward the exit.

In the spacious hallway several small groups are standing about, discussing the day's proceedings. Thomas McKean, chatting with the men from New Jersey, catches sight of John Adams and excuses himself to have a few words with the delegate from Massachusetts.

By tomorrow, Colonel McKean tells Adams, he is certain that Delaware will be on record in favor of independence. George Read, of course, will never change his mind—he's been saying no since the day he was born. Besides, his friendship with John Dickinson will never allow him to vote for independence. But Caesar Rodney should be here tomorrow—and he will cast the decisive vote for Delaware.

Adams want to know why Rodney has failed to appear today. McKean explains that there has been trouble in Sussex County. Now that Lord Howe is reportedly soon to arrive in New York, the Tories have been raising battalions to assist the British. Rodney, as the organizer of the Delaware militia, has been riding through the countryside, recruiting men to put down Tory uprisings.

McKean is confident that the express rider he dispatched in midafternoon will get through to Dover all right and deliver his urgent message to Rodney. Adams nods knowingly. So that was why McKean slipped out of the meeting room this afternoon earlier. The Delaware delegate explains, too, that this is entirely a personal appeal. He has paid the express rider out of his own pocket.

There's further good news. Ned Rutledge has told

McKean, only moments ago, that the South Carolina delegation has agreed to vote affirmatively tomorrow "for the sake of unanimity." A smile spreads across Adams' face. The cause of independence begins to look more promising. With the New York delegates appealing for revised instructions from their home assembly, only Pennsylvania remains in opposition.

Outside the heavy downpour has turned Chestnut Street into a tangle of mired carriages. Limping down the front steps, Dr. Franklin is thankful that his faithful parolees are there with the sedan chair, that his transportation will be along the brick footways and not through the maze of carriage traffic.

A number of delegates are making their way across the rain-washed cobblestones to Fountain Tavern, just opposite the State House. Rutledge and his group have agreed to meet at the City Tavern—where the management is always solicitous about providing a special room for their consultations.

President Hancock's sumptuous carriage, now slightly mud-spattered, has just pulled away from the curbing. He leans forward, urging the driver to hurry.

There will be a number of parties tonight in the brick homes that line both sides of High Street. Wealthy residents enjoy feting the delegates, but John Adams has had no invitations. There was a time, when he first arrived in Philadelphia, that he was besieged

with requests to attend the dinners of the conservatives—the Cadwaladers, the Whartons, the Mifflins. Now that he has become tagged as an "independence man," all invitations have ceased. The fact that he is "suspected" is of little consequence to John Adams. He is much too busy to be sociable anyway. Tonight there is a Board of War meeting, and after that he must stop by the Marine Committee.

Over at Tun Tavern, near the Walnut Street Wharf, Samuel Adams is entertaining John Morton at dinner. In his hometown of Boston, Sam Adams has made a habit of hanging around the waterfront, cultivating the sailors, the fishermen, the caulkers, and

riggers. Since coming to Philadelphia, he has followed the same practice. He is far more at ease in Tun Tavern than he would be in one of the more respectable eating establishments.

Sam Adams knows that, as a member of the Pennsylvania delegation, Morton's vote may be very important tomorrow. There are rumors that John Dickinson and Robert Morris may decide to stay away rather than face tomorrow's vote. With Benjamin Franklin and James Wilson certain to vote "Aye," with Charles Humphreys and Thomas Willing unalterably opposed, John Morton could break the tie for Pennsylvania.

Although a man of modest background, John Morton has held high office in Pennsylvania, serving several terms as speaker of the Pennsylvania Assembly. Now, for almost a year, he has followed the lead of his good friend John Dickinson, hoping for reconciliation with the mother country. His conservative friends have urged him to be cautious. They have warned him that if he votes for independence he'll be putting his family, as well as his future, into jeopardy. During the last few days Morton has begun to waver. Acutely aware of his responsibilities as a public servant, he is having difficulty making up his mind.

Sam Adams can ill afford to spend the money, but he feels he must make this eleventh-hour attempt to convert the conscientious Morton. Adams is adroit at persuasion—never pushing too far, never losing his temper. For the most part, however, the meal is not a success. The tavern tonight is unusually noisy. Boisterous seamen swarming into their water-front hangout make conversation difficult. As soon as dinner is over, Morton shakes hands with his host and departs, leaving Sam Adams to wonder whether anything he has said will affect Morton's vote tomorrow.

Five miles north of Philadelphia at Fairhill, John Dickinson is dining with his mother and his wife, Mary. Devoted as they are to this son and husband, both women understand from his silence that tonight

John is faced with a problem that he alone must decide. They would like to question him about it, perhaps offer some solution. But the tense expression on his face does not encourage conversation. Whatever happened today will not be disclosed; John Dickinson will never repeat one word that has been spoken behind those closed doors on Chestnut Street.

Immediately after President Hancock's dismissal this afternoon, Robert Morris cornered Dickinson. Morris has made up his mind, he tells Dickinson. Rather than agree to anything so rash as independence, he will stay away from tomorrow's session. During their hurried chat, Dickinson does not commit himself. He wants more time to explore the possibilities.

Now seated at the dining table, the head of the household merely minces with his food. His mind is racing through the day's events. It looks, indeed, as if the majority of delegates are about to go along with John Adams, forsaking the leadership of the man who is devoted to peace and reconciliation.

Among the hesitant are some who fear that by voting for independence, they will be signing their own death warrant. If the present rebellion is not successful—and there's little reason to believe it will be—the British Crown will have a list of men who can be convicted of high treason. Such a fear, however, has never

conditioned John Dickinson's thinking. His sole reason for failing to concur with those pressing for independence is based on his horror of violence. A large
majority of his fellow delegates are on the verge of
voting for independence. Yet he cannot, in good conscience, commit himself to something in which he
does not believe.

Abruptly, without a word, John Dickinson pushes
himself away from the table and goes quickly to his
bedroom. His decision has been made. As a colonel
in the First Regiment of Philadelphia, he will ride at
the head of his battalion tomorrow when they set out
for New York to offer assistance to General Washington. Now he must pack—his uniforms, his military cloak, his sword. And the stableman must be
notified to have his horse ready early tomorrow morning.

It's getting late, but there's still one further matter
which must be attended to. Going to his desk, Dickinson pulls out a bulky folder of papers. Tonight he
must sort them out, destroy anything that could bring
recrimination upon his family. He may be gone many
months—perhaps forever.

As he looks through the documents, memories flood
his mind—remembrances of his days as a young lawyer, a rising politician. All the acclaim he received as
the author of *Letters from a Farmer in Pennsylvania*.

And more recently, his business in the Continental Congress. Today he has made his final plea, but his heart-felt convictions have not been enough to sway his fellow delegates. Very well. Let them settle the issue of independence as their individual consciences dictate. His decision is made—and with it has come a measure of relief. Joining General Washington is the honorable way for a man of integrity to prove to his colleagues that he loves America as much as anyone.

At bricklayer Graff's second-floor apartment, the oil lamp in the parlor is burning late tonight. A steady scratching of a quill pen is the only sound in the room. Writing box propped on his knees, Thomas Jefferson is making copies of the declaration he placed on Secretary Thomson's desk last Friday. Two are completed—and the third one is nearly finished.

It has been a long evening's work. If the resolution for independence is adopted tomorrow, Jefferson knows that his distinguished colleagues will want to have their say about the paper he has drafted. There will be changes—probably many of them. Before any alteration is made, the determined young man wants his friends at home to know exactly where he stands. George Wythe, Patrick Henry, and Richard Henry Lee will all receive copies of his original draft.

Now he has reached the last sentence: "And for the

support of this Declaration, we mutually pledge to each other our lives, our fortunes, & our sacred honour." Noble words, these—words to show the world that this new nation's greatest strength lies in her citizens' faith in the future.

Relieved that his task is finished, Mr. Jefferson puts his pen back in the drawer, folds up his writing box, and moves to the open window. Rain has been falling intermittently through the evening, but now all is quiet. There is only the pungent odor of damp shrubbery mingled with the delicate fragrance of summer flowers. Muted flashes of lightning, thunderheads on the southern horizon indicate the storm is moving down into Delaware.

Peering out through the countryside, he ponders the possibilities for unanimity at the State House tomorrow. Can the fearful, the hesitant, the timid be won over in the few short hours that remain? Will these fifty-odd delegates be bold enough to declare themselves free of the mother country? Mr. Jefferson has high hopes that they will.

The Second of July

★★ 6 ★★

RODNEY'S WILD RIDE

It is almost one o'clock on this stormy morning of July second when the express rider whom Colonel McKean dispatched from Philadelphia yesterday afternoon gallops into Dover, Delaware. Approaching the village green, he brings his horse to a halt in front of the King George Tavern.

Yes, this must be the place. McKean said there would be a light in the window. And a sudden flash of lightning reveals the likeness of his Majesty on the sign above. Here he is to get specific directions about how to reach Rodney's farm.

The startled tavern keeper volunteers that Caesar Rodney lives on an 800-acre plantation, Byfield, about a mile and a half inland from Delaware Bay. Go straight ahead on the Kitts Hammock Road, he directs, and turn left at the first fork. The rider bolts out the door, mounts his horse with a leap, and disappears into the swirling rain, leaving the tavern keeper to wonder why, at this unearthly hour, a drenched express rider is trying to find Caesar Rodney.

The directions are simple enough, and within a short time the messenger has located the rambling wooden farmhouse set back on a shallow hill. Dismounting from his horse, he runs up the front steps and pounds on the door. Within minutes a night-shirted figure comes down the stairway, a lantern swinging from his hand, a musket tucked under his arm. The door opens cautiously. By the dim glow of the lantern, the rider sees a tall thin man standing before him, a gruesome disfigurement marring the left side of his face.

Shivering with exhaustion, the water-soaked rider explains that he has ridden all the way from Philadelphia with a dispatch from Colonel McKean. At the mention of his good friend's name, Rodney insists that the messenger come inside.

The rider apologizes for his late arrival—he's been delayed by the storm. But Colonel McKean is most anxious that Mr. Rodney come to the State House at once.

The cryptic message needs no further explanation. Rodney understands. George Read cannot be persuaded to alter his stand. This very day the vote for independence is to be taken, and Rodney is needed to break Delaware's tie vote. Delaware *must* be recorded as favoring independence. It's eighty-six miles to Philadelphia—storming, too. There's not a moment to lose.

The sound of voices brings the other members of the household downstairs. Briefly Caesar Rodney explains the urgency of his trip to his brother, Tom, and asks that the rider be made comfortable for what's left of the night. And will his nephew please saddle the swiftest roan in the stable?

Disappearing upstairs, Rodney is back within minutes, throwing on his leather jacket, adjusting the silver spurs on his boots. Pulling a light-green silk scarf from his pocket, he wraps it around his neck and across the left side of his face—something he always does before appearing in public. Meticulous about his personal appearance, Rodney has no wish to offend anyone with the sight of the cancer that is eating away his left cheek.

Now he is hurrying out the door. The horse is ready. Rodney mounts quickly, digs his spurs into the roan's flanks, and speeds off through the pitch-blackness.

The forty-seven-year-old bachelor from Kent County has spent most of his life on the plantation he inherited from his father. Public-spirited, interested in colonial affairs, he has been active in the Delaware legislature. Seven years ago he was elected speaker of the lower house. He's also served as his colony's chairman on the Committee of Correspondence.

Just two years ago Rodney was given a brigadier general's commission and asked to command Delaware's militia. It has been a challenge. The colony is filled with Loyalists. He has had to ride the length and breadth of Delaware, recruiting volunteers willing to serve in the militia. Nonetheless, the men under his command are known as a well-trained, finely disciplined group.

Fortunately Rodney is thoroughly familiar with the countryside. Through this early-morning tempest, the trail is not easy to follow. He crisscrosses around the sand dunes and marshes along Delaware Bay, heading northward. Only when zigzag streaks of lightning brighten the sky can Rodney see where he is going.

At Smyrna he picks up the wagon road, dignified by the title of King's Highway. On toward Blackbird he plunges, half-riding, half-swimming through the torrent of water that is Appoquinimink Creek. Leaning far forward, Rodney drives his horse hard, but the sticky mire of Delaware's sandy soil slows the going.

A sudden gust of wind lashes the rider's face with the force of a strong whip. Instinctively Rodney reaches up to adjust the green silk handkerchief over

his face. His doctors have urged him to go to London for surgery to relieve the incessant pain. Close friends, concerned about his health, have been quick to point out that if he votes for independence, such a trip will be impossible. Rodney knows this. He's never given it a second thought.

Between five and six the first streaks of a gray dawn break the blackness of the night. Now the wind dies down. The rain becomes only an intermittent dripping. Rodney is bent low in the saddle, he and the horse moving as one swift being. There are many more miles to cover, but the roan is now out in the open, running free and fast.

Hare's Corner—Rodney has come more than forty miles. And six miles further—Wilmington. Plunging along the main thoroughfare of the little market town, the horse's hooves beat a sharp tattoo on the rough cobblestones. The old Dutch and Swedish settlers gasp at the mud-caked rider who gallops through their village, looking to neither right nor left.

Leaving Wilmington, Rodney continues on to Claymont, stopping at the Queen of France Tavern only long enough to secure a fresh mount. On and on he gallops, driven by his desperate desire to reach Philadelphia before Delaware's vote is cast. It's less than forty miles now. He must make up for those hours lost earlier in the storm.

★★ 7 ★★

AND NOW, MR. LEE'S RESOLUTION

Dark clouds, scudding across the sky, hold a threat of more wet weather for Philadelphia on this early Tuesday morning. There has been rain, off and on, throughout the night, washing away most of yesterday's mud on the cobblestone streets. But the humidity is still high. There are signs that a new storm may be moving in from the south. By six A.M., as many of the delegates are setting out for various committee meetings, the thermometer registers an oppressive 70 degrees.

In his room at Mrs. Yard's, John Adams is already making notes for the other members on the Board of War. As chairman, he has put in long hours of work. Congress has no authority to make any specific demands, and Mr. Adams has found that gearing thirteen separate colonies for the business of war is a slow and discouraging process. Procuring ammunition has been time-consuming. Just last week he was able to locate men to set up an iron foundry. He has also recruited workers for a musket factory here in Philadelphia. Production has already started—eventually they hope to manufacture twenty-five muskets a day.

Promptly at eight o'clock, Mr. Adams receives a visit from his barber, Mr. Burne. The man is anxious to talk, perhaps to gather a bit of gossip about what's been happening at the State House. All Philadelphia is curious. It would be quite a feather in his cap if he could only ferret out a piece of news to pass on to his next client.

But John Adams remains strangely silent as he is lathered and shaved. He has no intention of being drawn into a conversation that might divulge the dissension of the past few weeks. Until the issue of independence is settled, one way or another, the outside world must know nothing.

Once the barber has gone, John Adams stuffs his notes into his green cloth satchel and sets out for the State House. The short stocky man, dressed all in black, hurries along Chestnut Street, occasionally clutching his three-cornered hat as small gusts of wind threaten to send it sailing across the street. The motion is involuntary; Adams is mentally checking off the delegates, colony by colony. Many of those in Congress have voiced their frank opinion, either for or against independence. Those votes are easy to tabulate. But there are a few timid souls who waver from hour to hour. Which direction will they take today? Until the delegates have accepted Mr. Lee's resolution, there is no point in thinking of the paper Mr. Jefferson has submitted.

At bricklayer Graff's, Thomas Jefferson is about to leave for the State House. He folds up his writing box on the parlor table, tucking two small volumes into the bottom drawer. An insatiable reader, Jefferson frequently borrows books from Benjamin Franklin's Free Library Company of Philadelphia. The library, now located in Carpenter's Hall, is easily accessible; members of the Second Continental Congress have been encouraged to use its valuable collection of books. Since space has not permitted him to bring to Philadelphia many books from his own library, Mr. Jefferson has especially appreciated this privilege. This morning he intends to start early enough to drop off these two books at Carpenter's Hall before going on to the State House.

It is now shortly before nine o'clock, and the delegates have begun filing into their meeting room in groups of twos and threes. Some are visibly nervous, others impatient and irritable. The New England men glance around the room with anxious eyes, scanning the faces of all present. Can the rumor be true that John Dickinson and Robert Morris will not be here today? If Pennsylvania's archconservatives have agreed to absent themselves, perhaps the tide for independence can be turned, after all.

John Alsop, head of the New York delegation, has already gathered the other members of his group around him—George Clinton, Francis Lewis, Henry Wisner, and William Floyd. The men realize that their position more and more presents a dilemma. They have sent message after message to the New York Assembly, asking for instructions. They dare not vote as individuals, each man according to his conscience. They must wait for new instructions. Until that word comes, the delegates agree to abstain from voting.

As the clock in the tower strikes nine, President Hancock raps his gavel and calls the meeting to order. There are the usual reports and dispatches to be read. A letter from General Washington contains grave news: "When I had the honor of addressing you Yesterday, I had only been informed of the arrival of Forty Five of the Fleet in the morning; since then I have received Authentic Intelligence from sundry persons, among them from General Greene, that one hundred and ten sails came in before Night, that they were counted, and that more were seen about dusk in the offing."

John Adams in his front-row seat listens intently. How can anyone, after hearing this news, believe there can still be reconciliation with the British? His colleagues must realize that war is already an established fact, that a declaration of independence by Congress will unite the colonies as nothing else can.

Outside the rain has begun, a steady downpour that necessitates closing of all the windows, even at the top. The air in the room grows stifling.

There are further reports, bills to be paid, assignments made to committee members. As President Hancock continues reading, a number of the New England delegates are making silent computations. The rumor must be true—John Dickinson and Robert Morris have not put in an appearance. Both the lawyer and the merchant are habitually punctual. Surely if they were planning to come, they would be here by now. John Adams, knowing that Colonel McKean has sent for Caesar Rodney, wonders what has delayed the delegate from Delaware.

The minutes pass and become hours, hours consumed by routine business. President Hancock is aware of the importance of Rodney's arrival. As a delaying tactic, he is bringing up matters that he knows will cause argument.

Meanwhile Colonel McKean slips out of the room every little while to pace up and down in front of the State House. It's almost three o'clock, and there's still no sign of any horseback rider. Perhaps his fellow delegate has been unable to get through the storm after all.

The Marine Committee asks the advice of the delegates about two naval officers—Abraham Whipple and Dudley Saltonstall—who are charged with "insubordination and malpractice." There is further argument about what should be done, argument carried on primarily by the New Englanders. Word has been passed around that Caesar Rodney is on his way. The question of independence must be put off as long as possible.

The afternoon wears on; the delegates become more and more uneasy. Glancing apprehensively at the clock, President Hancock realizes that he can delay matters no longer. It is now after four o'clock. He must resolve Congress once more into a committee of the whole. With elaborate ceremony, he sets aside the mace and yields the chair to Benjamin Harrison.

Mr. Harrison asks Secretary Thomson to repeat Mr. Lee's resolution once more before the final roll call. The secretary leafs back through the Journal of

Congress until he locates the entry made on June seventh. In measured tones he reads the resolution proposing that all connection with the mother country be dissolved, that the colonies declare themselves free and independent states.

While Secretary Thomson is reading, Colonel McKean once again slips from the room. Taking up a watch on the steps outside, he anxiously scans the street.

Not a word is uttered when the secretary finishes. The room is silent, tense with uncertainty. Mr. Harrison nods to Thomson, and the roll call begins.

"New Hampshire . . . Massachusetts . . . Connecticut . . . Rhode Island." All the New Englanders reply with a vigorous "Aye."

"New York . . ." The New York delegates state that they have agreed to abstain from voting.

"New Jersey." Their affirmative vote, as expected, is unanimous. These are the new delegates, "high-charged with independence."

Now it is Pennsylvania's turn. Secretary Thomson asks for Franklin's vote and receives a hearty "Aye." James Wilson has finally resolved his doubts and responds in the affirmative. Charles Humphreys and Thomas Willing are still opposed. The fifth vote will be John Morton's—his to break the deadlock for Pennsylvania, either for or against.

For a long moment Morton remains seated, his eyes on the floor. There were months when he was so certain; he followed John Dickinson's lead, believing that peace above all else was important. Yet within the last few weeks he has begun to have doubts, and last night Sam Adams was very persuasive. Now that the threat of Howe's armada is hovering over New York City, Britain seems to be offering peace only at the point of a bayonet. White-faced, John Morton gets to his feet and casts his vote in the affirmative, officially committing Pennsylvania to the cause of independence.

Outside the State House, Colonel McKean is still straining his eyes in search of a rider on horseback. He can wait no longer. Rodney has not been able to get through the storm. In despair McKean turns toward the doorway. Suddenly, there's the most welcome sound in the world—the swift clatter of a horse's hoofs on the cobblestones. Whirling about, McKean watches the approaching rider, a man so bespattered by mud as to be almost unrecognizable.

Caesar Rodney brings his horse to an abrupt halt, dismounts, and runs up the steps. Breathlessly he explains he's been delayed by the storm, but he hopes he is still in time. McKean nods reassuringly, and the two men walk into the hallway together.

The creaking of the door causes a stir among the delegates. Heads turn toward the back of the room

as the two men make their entrance. Beside Colonel McKean is a man still booted and spurred, his face drawn with fatigue, his eyes hollow from lack of sleep. Everyone recognizes Caesar Rodney, the delegate whom John Adams once described as "the oddest-looking man in the world; he is tall, thin and slender as a reed, pale; his face is not bigger than a large apple, yet there is sense and fire, spirit, wit and humor in his countenance."

Now Secretary Thomson is asking for Delaware's vote. Colonel McKean calls out a triumphant "Aye," though his vote is promptly negated by that of George Read. Caesar Rodney is next. Coming forward to face the delegates, Rodney responds by saying, "As I believe the voice of my constituents and of all sensible and honest men is in favor of independence and my own judgment concurs with them, I vote for independence." Delaware's vote is recorded as affirmative.

The roll call continues. Maryland—in accordance with the instructions received yesterday morning— votes for the resolution. Virginia, of course, has always been solidly behind it. Many weeks ago the Virginia Convention dispatched to its delegates the following message: "We instruct you positively to declare for independency; that you solemnly abjure any allegiance to His Britannic Majesty, and bid him a good night forever."

Edward Rutledge, though he still doesn't like the idea, has been true to his word. He has swung the South Carolina delegation to an affirmative vote "for the sake of unanimity." North Carolina's delegates follow the lead of their sister state; Georgia has backed the resolution from the beginning.

Secretary Thomson whispers the final tally to Mr. Harrison. The committee of the whole is dissolved, and President Hancock resumes the chair, carefully replacing the silver mace.

Following the parliamentary rules set up by the Congress, Mr. Harrison addresses the president, reporting that twelve colonies have voted—twelve colonies favor independence. With the report of the committee of the whole before them, the delegates formally adopt Mr. Lee's resolution.

Whatever the emotions the delegates are experiencing, there is no display. No cheers arise. The moment is too solemn for any celebration, this moment on July 2, 1776, when the resolution for independence becomes an accomplished fact. No longer separate colonies under his Majesty's rule, they are henceforth to be one united country—the United States of America.

The tension of the long day is evident. The delegates are impatient for dismissal although Mr. Harrison has one final detail. He reports that the committee of the whole has not had time to go over the draft of the declaration on independence submitted by Mr. Jefferson and requests permission for the committee to sit again tomorrow.

In his Journal of Congress, Secretary Thomson dutifully records: "Resolved, that this Congress will, tomorrow, again resolve itself into a Committee of the Whole, to take into consideration the declaration on independence."

President Hancock orders an adjournment until nine o'clock tomorrow morning.

★★ 8 ★★

THE EVENING HOURS

"The happy, the peaceful, the elegant, the hospitable and polite city of Philadelphia" is completely unaware of the momentous step that has just been taken at the State House. As the delegates emerge from the meeting room, there is no hint of riotous celebration.

People strolling along the footways see only a weary-looking group of men—collars wilted, waistcoats and breeches disheveled by the humidity of the stifling room. They disperse quickly, with little conversation. The thing is over, done with. There's no need for further politicking among themselves. And—until Mr. Jefferson's declaration is officially adopted—no one must know what has occurred in the white-paneled room.

Hurrying away from the State House, John Adams swings briskly along the brick footways of Chestnut Street, his eyes bright with the victory of today's session. As soon as he enters his sparsely furnished room at Mrs. Yard's, Adams goes to work. There are reports to be completed, letters to be written. But even as he writes, John Adams has sobering thoughts. This day's triumph—the passing of Mr. Lee's resolution—can only bring new dangers to his little family at Braintree. He knows, nonetheless, that his courageous Abby would not have it otherwise.

The quiet of the room is broken abruptly by the sound of bells. It must be the bells in Christ Church pealing out their weekly message—that tomorrow, Wednesday, is market day in Philadelphia. The "butter bells" people call them. Back home in Boston, Adams recalls, they blow a conch instead. But Philadelphia is an unusual city.

The very design of the city is unlike any other in the colonies. It was planned by William Penn, more than three generations ago. A "Holy Experiment," he called it, a place of refuge for the persecuted Quakers of England. Every detail was plotted out, worked over, amended. Its streets, in particular, interest John Adams. In sharp contrast to the narrow, winding thoroughfares of Boston, these streets are laid out in strict parallels, bisected by equally parallel cross streets—

almost like a checkerboard. The street names, so John has written Abigail, are taken "from forest and fruit trees—Pear Street, Apple Street, Walnut Street, Chestnut Street."

Over at City Tavern tonight a number of the delegates have gathered to exchange rumors and confidences about the plot to assassinate General Washington, a plot uncovered less than two weeks ago.

The colony of New York has long been known to be filled with Tories. But to find traitors within General Washington's own forces—this is unbelievably shocking. According to the news which has filtered down to Philadelphia, the plot was carefully drawn. As soon as Lord Howe's fleet of ships gathered in New York Harbor, a signal was to be given. Then the traitors within the Continental army would begin firing on their own troops. One rumor had it that Washington was to be shot by a member of his own bodyguard. A contradictory story was told that the general was to be kidnapped and taken aboard a British ship to be tried for treason.

Fortunately the scheme was discovered after Sergeant Thomas Hickey, one of Washington's favorite bodyguards, was picked up for trying to pass counterfeit money at Hull's Tavern. While in jail, Hickey began bragging about how many soldiers in Washington's army were not in sympathy with the cause for which they were supposed to be fighting. One of the prisoners overheard Hickey and reported his traitorous words to the New York Assembly.

A three-man committee was immediately appointed by the Assembly, but when the members visited Hickey in his jail cell, they failed to gain any information from him. After further investigation they picked up the trail of a gunsmith, Gilbert Forbes, who had been recruiting for the British. Forbes was told that less than a week before, Congress had passed a resolution which made treason a crime punishable by hanging. To save his neck, Forbes confessed that he had recruited men from Washington's own guard and that Hickey had been one of them.

Reports of the findings were given to General Washington just last Wednesday morning. The general acted immediately; a court-martial was held within hours. Hickey was judged guilty and sentenced to hang that Friday, June 28. After the traitor's death, General Washington posted the following order: "The unhappy fate of Thomas Hickey, executed this day for mutiny, sedition, and treachery, the General hopes will be a warning to every soldier in the army to avoid those crimes and all others, so disgraceful to the character of a soldier and pernicious to the country whose pay he receives and bread he eats. . . ."

In his apartment at Seventh and Market Streets, Thomas Jefferson is reviewing the day's events. Victory has been won—yes; but there is still his draft of the declaration to consider. The members of Congress can be a cantankerous lot. He's heard many of them express definite ideas about literary style—and they'll be meticulous about content, too. Tonight the author senses that his fellow delegates will not be as kindly disposed toward his composition as Mr. Franklin, Mr. Sherman, and Mr. Adams.

There's comfort in the thought that once the text of the declaration is agreed upon—and adopted— Congress will face the world as a united body. Independence will be an accomplished fact for the thirteen new states, but a useless fact unless it can be backed up by victory in the field. At this moment the prospects are not too promising.

A bold thrust into Canada has failed because Benedict Arnold's troops lacked the necessary reinforcements. General Burgoyne's soldiers have driven the Americans back down Lake Champlain, a staggering blow that has left Canada wide open.

General Washington's report that a great fleet is gathering in New York Harbor has alarming implications. And in the South there's been an attempt to capture the port of Charleston, South Carolina. General Charles Lee has been sending emphatic pleas to

Congress for reinforcements. But during the past week there has been no further word from the beleaguered South.

It now appears that the British military strategy involves a three-pronged attack. Invasion from the north, south, and east—if executed simultaneously—could deliver a knockout blow. Should General Washington's forces be captured, the port of New York could become a beachhead. By cutting off the North from the South, by separating New England from the Middle Colonies, the British would sever all means of communication. The colonists would have little choice but to surrender.

Dismal as the prospects appear, Thomas Jefferson is confident that America will not so easily be conquered. The men who have voted for independence today are the country's leaders. They have spoken for the three million inhabitants of a new nation. It may take time, but surely with General Washington in command the Revolutionary War will eventually end in victory.

The Third of July

★★ 9 ★★

MORNING
PRELIMINARIES

Early on the morning of July third the weather is "fine, clear, and cool," according to the notes which Thomas Jefferson records in his diary. There's a refreshing breeze "blowing in from the north," hinting that the hot spell which has held Philadelphia in its grip for the past week may well be broken.

John Adams is back at his desk before six o'clock. His style in writing public documents is apt to be ponderous, but his diaries, his letters to his family and friends, give vivid accounts of events that have stirred his emotions. Still exuberant from yesterday's triumph, he shares his thoughts this morning with his beloved Abby:

"The second of July, 1776," he writes, "will be the most memorable epocha in the history of America. I am apt to believe that it will be celebrated by succeeding generations as the great anniversary festival. It ought to be commemorated as the day of deliverance, by solemn acts of devotion to God Almighty. It ought to be solemnized with pomp and parade, with shows, games, sports, guns, bells, bonfires, and illuminations, from one end of this continent to the other, from this time forward forevermore. . . ."

A little before nine the members of Congress begin converging on the State House. Habitually punctual, Dr. Franklin limps into the meeting room to take his place in the back row beside Thomas Jefferson. Around the president's table on the dais, a number of delegates are holding a heated discussion.

Curious about what's going on, Dr. Franklin asks Mr. Jefferson for an explanation. It seems that when Secretary Thomson arrived a few minutes ago, he found an anonymous note on the table. He handed it to Mr. Harrison who read the threat aloud: "You have gone too far. Take care. A plot is framed for your destruction and all of you shall be destroyed."

Secretary Thomson is sure that this is the work of a practical jokester, but others are expressing genuine consternation. Everyone knows that Philadelphia is full of potential enemies—with Loyalists who would

go to almost any lengths for King George. Perhaps word has leaked out that this is the day when the terms for the declaration will be debated.

Fidgety Elbridge Gerry from Massachusetts wonders if there may not be a bomb planted somewhere in the building. The cellar, he suggests, should be searched, at least that part of the cellar which is under the room where Congress is sitting. After all, it is less than two weeks ago since the plot to kill General Washington was uncovered. Benjamin Harrison and Carter Braxton agree with Mr. Gerry and volunteer to lead a search party.

Some of the delegates are obviously bored with the small uproar; others are smiling at the alarm caused by such a prank.

At this moment President Hancock stalks down the center aisle and makes his way to the dais. After glancing at the anonymous note, he tosses it aside. Threats like this one have been a daily part of his life ever since "the Boston Tea Party."

Mr. Gerry again asks that the cellar be searched. Before President Hancock can answer, Joseph Hewes of North Carolina is addressing the chair. He thinks that such a search would be a waste of time, that the note should be treated with contempt rather than a show of fear. Further he says, "I would almost as soon be blown up as to discover to the world that I think myself in danger." The staunch New Englanders applaud his show of courage.

President Hancock nods in agreement and brings down the gavel. The meeting comes to order. There are the usual dispatches and communications to be read. A letter from Augusta, Georgia, describes the troubles of the commissioners on Indian affairs and asks for expense money. The expense account is referred to the Board of Treasury.

The question of recruiting more men for "the Flying Camp" touches off a tedious discussion. Just last May twenty-ninth, Congress approved the plan for the Flying Camp, a group of some ten thousand militiamen from Pennsylvania, Maryland, and Delaware. The primary purpose of the group is to protect Philadelphia from any sudden enemy invasion. The Flying Camp is a small army that can act quickly without disrupting General Washington's troops based in New York. Plans call for the Camp's existence only until the end of September; the pay of the men will be the same as that of the regular Continental soldiers. So far, only three thousand men have joined. The delegates pass a resolution to send a circular letter to the colonies involved requesting more active recruiting. It is also decided to ask General Washington to appoint a commander.

There is consternation expressed that so far today

no word has been received from General Washington. Rumor has it that the city of New York has been overrun by the British. What's more, no one knows how many foreign mercenaries—soldiers who will fight anywhere for a specified sum of money—the British have been able to recruit from Germany. Some say the number of Hessians is overwhelming. If Washington cannot save the city, what is to stop the Redcoats from coming straight down to Philadelphia? The concern of the delegates makes John Hancock thankful that he is not holding General Washington's position. This has not always been so.

A little more than a year ago—on June 10, 1775, to be exact—John Adams addressed the newly assembled delegates of the Second Continental Congress in Carpenter's Hall, describing the man whom they hoped to persuade to take over the job of commander in chief. Hancock listened expectantly, certain that his was the name which John Adams was about to propose. When George Washington was nominated instead, Hancock was bitterly disappointed.

The day after his formal election, the quiet Virginia plantation owner in the blue-and-buff colonel's uniform addressed his fellow delegates. He thanked them for the honor they had given him and remarked that although his ability was unequal to the trust they had placed in him he would do everything in his power to support the cause for which they were fighting. He closed by saying: "I beg it may be remembered by every gentleman in the room that I this day declare with utmost sincerity: I do not think myself equal to the command I am honored with."

In the months that followed, John Hancock's humiliation had begun to dissolve. Disappointment for himself had changed to admiration for the commander in chief. When Washington was forcing the British to withdraw from Boston last March, Hancock had written him: "I am determined to serve under you—if it be to take the firelock and join the ranks as a volunteer."

This morning the uncertainty about Howe's approaching armada has made the delegates even more apprehensive. How many troops will land in New York? And how strong are they? Any news, even bad news, from Washington's headquarters would be better than no word at all.

There are more reports from committees. Among them a request from Benedict Arnold asking for more shipwrights at Crown Point. The men are needed at once. The delegates decide that the Marine Committee should be empowered to contract for these marine carpenters who will go to Lake Champlain and build a fleet there, a fleet which it is hoped will help keep the British in Canada. It is also agreed that each car-

penter will be paid at the rate of "thirty-four and two-thirds dollars per month" plus one and a half rations and a half pint of rum a day.

Seated in the back row, Thomas Jefferson is becoming increasingly nervous. "He sits in a lounging manner," one of his colleagues has commented, "on one hip commonly, and with one of his shoulders elevated much above the other." Despite his relaxed posture, Mr. Jefferson feels tension rising within him.

On this Wednesday morning there are endless reports, so much talk, before his draft comes before the delegates. A smile of encouragement from old Dr. Franklin, himself an author, proves the elderly diplomat understands the doubts that are filling Mr. Jefferson's mind.

★★ *10* ★★

THE DEBATE BEGINS

It is nearly one o'clock before President Hancock hands the silver mace to Secretary Thomson and the assembly once again resolves itself into a committee of the whole, Benjamin Harrison assuming the president's chair.

Reaching for Mr. Jefferson's fair copy, Mr. Harrison hands it to Secretary Thomson. Thomson reads fluently and well. His delivery, Harrison knows, will be far better than the chairman's own.

The secretary rises. In tones audible to every man in the room, he begins: "A Declaration by the Representatives of the UNITED STATES OF AMERICA, in General Congress assembled." This is the first time the thirteen colonies have been referred to as the United States of America in a public document. It has an unfamiliar sound.

First comes the preamble: "When in the course of human events it becomes necessary for one people to dissolve the political bands which have connected them with another, and to assume among the powers of the earth the separate and equal station to which the laws of nature and of nature's god entitle them, a decent respect to the opinions of mankind requires that they should declare the causes which impel them to the separation." The delegates nod in agreement. This is a good beginning.

Secretary Thomson now begins the second paragraph, the statement of general political philosophy which sets forth the moral and legal justification for separation from the mother country: "We hold these truths to be self-evident; that all men are created equal; that they are endowed by their creator with inherent and inalienable rights; that among these are life, liberty, and the pursuit of happiness; that to secure these rights, governments are instituted among men, deriving their just powers from the consent of the governed. . . ." The secretary continues reading until he reaches the close of the paragraph.

Now that he has reached the end of the first page, Mr. Thomson pauses. The delegates are quick with their criticisms. Several changes are proposed, primarily to clarify the meaning. "Inherent and inalienable rights" is changed to read "certain inalienable rights." The word "expunge" becomes "alter." "Unremitting injuries" is revised to read "repeated injuries." The delegates are practical men, intent on altering anything that seems too ornate.

In the final sentence of the second paragraph, Mr. Jefferson has written: "To prove this, let facts be submitted to a candid world, for the truth of which we pledge a faith yet unsullied by falsehood."

There is a murmur of disagreement among the delegates. Isn't it slightly absurd to hold up this new nation's reputation as completely "unsullied by falsehood"? In his writing the author has seemed to endow the colonies with an almost saintlike purity. The delegates are realists, and they object to such a sanctimonious aura.

One of the delegates reminds the assembly that this document is something that all the world will soon be reading. There will be many people, he points out, who will be more than anxious to criticize, to search out errors and misstatements. Therefore, would it not be better to tone down some of Mr. Jefferson's "flights of fancy" and present an accurate, factual statement of their position?

The offending phrase is stricken. Secretary Thomson alters the draft to read: "To prove this, let facts be submitted to a candid world."

With the first two paragraphs now approved, the secretary begins to read the list of specific grievances against the king:

He has refused his assent to laws the most wholesome and necessary for the public good.

He has forbidden his governors to pass laws of immediate & pressing importance, unless suspended in their operation till his assent should be obtained; and when so suspended, he has neglected utterly to attend to them. . . .

The delegates are stern editors, none too tactful at times. Line by line, they debate the charges. Isn't this passage too severe? Can that phrase be misconstrued? Whenever the debate threatens to become too lengthy, John Adams leaps to his feet to defend his young friend's words. Years later, Mr. Jefferson would write that Adams "was the pillar of its [the Declaration's] support on the floor of Congress, its ablest advocate and defender of the multifarious assaults it encountered."

In a number of instances, the delegates' changes are an improvement over what Mr. Jefferson has written. The eighth charge, that "he has suffered the administration of justice totally to cease in some of these

states, refusing his assent to laws for establishing judiciary powers," becomes clearer after correction. The word "suffered" is changed to "obstructed" and "totally to cease in some of these states" is deleted. Now it will read: "He has obstructed the administration of justice by refusing his assent to laws for establishing judiciary powers."

The tenth indictment—"he has erected a multitude of new offices by a self-assumed power & sent hither swarms of officers to harrass our people & eat out their substance"—is toned down by taking out the phrase "by a self-assumed power."

Many in Congress do not approve of the phraseology in the fourteenth charge. Mr. Jefferson has written, "he has abdicated government here, withdrawing his governors & declaring us out of his allegiance and protection." After some discussion the delegates agree that this grievance will be more effective if it reads, "he has abdicated government here, by declaring us out of his protection and waging war against us."

From his back-row seat, Thomas Jefferson is listening in silent embarrassment. His carefully worked phrases are being twisted and turned, questioned, mutilated. It is a harrowing experience for a sensitive man. Beside him, Dr. Franklin leans over and puts a comforting hand on the the young man's knee.

"I have made it a rule," says the sympathetic Frank-

lin, "whenever in my power, to avoid becoming the draughtsman of papers to be reviewed by a public body. I took my lesson from an incident which I will relate to you.

"When I was a journeyman printer," he continues, "one of my companions, an apprentice Hatter, having served out his time, was about to open a shop for himself. His first concern was to have a handsome signboard, with a proper inscription. He composed it in these words—'*John Thompson, Hatter, makes and sells hats for ready money*'—with a figure of a hat sub-joined, but he thought he would submit it to his friends for their amendments.

"The first he showed it to thought the word *Hatter* tautologous because followed by the words *makes hats* which showed he was a Hatter. It was struck out.

"The next observed that the word *makes* might as well be omitted, because his customers would not care who made the hats. If good and to their mind, they would buy, by whomsoever made. He struck it out.

"A third said he thought the words *for ready money* were useless as it was not the custom of the place to sell on credit. Everyone who purchased expected to pay. They were parted with, and the inscription now stood, *John Thompson sells hats.*

" '*Sells hats!*' says his next friend. 'Why nobody will expect you to *give* them away. What then is the use of that word?' It was stricken out, and *hats* followed it, the rather, as there was one painted on the board.

"So his inscription was reduced ultimately to *John Thompson* with the figure of a hat subjoined."

When Dr. Franklin finishes his little anecdote, Mr. Jefferson manages a wry smile. The impulse which has prompted the story is a kind one, and the author is touched by the old man's concern for his feelings.

Now Secretary Thomson is reading the final accusation against the Crown, the charge Mr. Jefferson has carefully reserved as a climax to the list of grievances— the enslavement of Negroes from North Africa. "He has waged cruel war against human nature itself, violating its most sacred rights of life & liberty in the persons of a distant people, who never offended him, captivating & carrying them into slavery in another hemisphere, or to incur miserable death in their transportation thither . . ."

Several of the Southern delegates have grave misgivings about such an indictment. Plantation owners are dependent on the slaves for working the fields of cotton and tobacco.

The secretary reads on: ". . . this piratical warfare, the opprobrium of *infidel* powers, is the warfare of the *Christian* king of Great Britain, determined to keep open a market where MEN should be bought & sold. . . ."

To point up his strong feeling against the slave trade, Mr. Jefferson, in his manuscript, has underlined the words "infidel" and "Christian." He has capitalized the word *men* so that it stands out boldly on the closely written sheet.

For more than a hundred years now, British traders have been capturing black men in Africa. They have jammed them into slave ships, transported them across the ocean, and sold them to plantation owners. Among the total population of approximately three million people now in America, there are nearly half a million Negroes. In several Southern counties, the black men outnumber the whites by twenty to one.

Many of the delegates are in sympathy with the sentiments expressed by Thomas Jefferson. Dr. Franklin, for one, has long advocated the abolition of slavery. He has sponsored the first free school for Negroes. With the exception of Georgia and South Carolina, all the colonies are actually opposed to the slave trade. Yet to include such an indictment in the Declaration is presuming a little too much.

Edward Rutledge leaps to his feet, declaring that slavery should be determined by the states themselves —not made a matter for Congress to decide. John Adams counters with a statement that slavery is weakening, not strengthening, the country.

Button Gwinnett, the delegate from Georgia, agrees that slavery may be wrong but insists that right now his colony is very dependent on slave labor. In time he thinks it will disappear.

The assembly room has become a veritable hornets' nest. Arguments fly back and forth. John Adams believes that slavery is not consistent with the principle that "all men are created equal"—and says so with vehemence. Rutledge is adamant; South Carolina will never agree to the Declaration unless this clause is removed. The delegation from Georgia stands firmly behind him.

Even as he read Mr. Jefferson's draft several weeks ago, John Adams feared that this passage might arouse bitter feelings. Now it has become a major stumbling block. Mr. Jefferson stirs uneasily in his chair. He has been so hopeful about this clause. He dreads to see it eliminated. Perhaps some compromise can be worked out. On the opposite side of the room, the shrewd Mr. Adams perceives that unity among the delegates is still uncertain. Indictment of the slave trade must not be allowed to wreck the patriots' cause.

As the afternoon wanes, there is still no agreement. President Hancock, noting that the hour for adjournment has arrived, resumes the president's chair. He proposes a resolution which is readily adopted: "That this Congress, will, tomorrow, resolve itself into a Committee of the Whole, to take into further consideration, the Declaration."

And Secretary Thomson inscribes in the Journal: "Adjourned to 9 o'clock tomorrow."

The Fourth of July

★★ *11* ★★

FURTHER
PROS AND CONS

An atmosphere of somber quiet pervades the State House meeting room as the members of the Second Continental Congress gather on this morning of July 4, 1776. Outside the sun is shining brightly. At a few minutes before nine the temperature stands at 72.5 degrees—a fact Mr. Jefferson meticulously jots down in his notes. A breeze from the southeast holds promise that today's humidity will be less suffocating than it was yesterday.

Outwardly calm, and seemingly oblivious to the tension in the room, President Hancock walks up the center aisle to take his chair on the dais. As the clock in the State House tower strikes nine, the president brings down his gavel, and the meeting is called to order.

Following routine procedure, the reports and bulletins are read first. From General Washington there
is an urgent appeal: "Our reinforcements of militia
are small as yet. I submit to Congress whether it may
not be expedient for them to repeat and press home
their requests to the different governments to furnish
their quotas with all possible dispatch."

Time and again, Mr. Hancock has written the various colonies, urging, pleading with them to send men
to the Continental army. However, Congress has no
real authority. Only the colonial assemblies themselves
can order men to report for duty. This morning President Hancock asks the delegates to get in touch with
their assemblies at once and explain General Washington's desperate position.

Doorman MacNair slips up to the dais and hands
President Hancock a communiqué, which has just
been delivered by special messenger. Unfolding the
paper, the president notes that it also is from General
Washington. He reads aloud: "I must entreat your
attention to an application I made some time ago for
flints. . . . We are extremely deficient in the necessary
article."

The gravity of the situation is apparent to all. With
Howe's armada sailing into New York Harbor at this
very moment, Pennsylvania must not be allowed to
hoard its stock of precious flints. A unanimous deci-

sion is made, and Secretary Thomson records in the Journal: "Resolved, That an application be made to the Committee of Safety of Pennsylvania for a supply of flints for the troops at New York. . . ."

The New England men, seated in the front row, stir restlessly, hopeful that the preliminaries will soon be ended. These bulletins from General Washington only serve to point up the need for swift action. There can be no further quibbling. The final step must be taken—and soon.

By midmorning the delegates have resolved themselves into committee-of-the-whole status. Chairman Harrison is now seated in the president's chair, to preside over the unfinished business of editing the declaration.

Resuming where they left off yesterday afternoon, the delegates take up the controversial slave indictment first. Thomas Jefferson is hoping fiercely that the clause will be allowed to stand. Virginia, Maryland, Pennsylvania, all make earnest appeals for it. But South Carolina and Georgia will not be budged from their original position. If the slave clause remains, these two states will never sign. To preserve the already precarious unity of Congress, there is only one course to take. The offending paragraph is deleted from the manuscript.

Heartsick, Thomas Jefferson marks out the slave

clause. Ever since the deliberations began, Mr. Jefferson has been following the rough draft which he has placed on his portable desk. Whenever a change is authorized, he makes it on his own paper—bracketing, interlining, and writing in the margins. This final charge, more than any of the others, was one he hoped to see included.

Now Secretary Thomson begins reading the last page—the paragraph preceding the actual declaration

of the act that will sever the colonies from the mother country. The delegates listen intently, waiting to pounce on any words which might misrepresent their purpose.

When the secretary reaches the sentence ". . . they are permitting their chief magistrate to send over not only soldiers of our common blood, but Scotch & foreign mercenaries to invade & destroy us . . . ," two members of Congress are on their feet at once. The Reverend Mr. Witherspoon and Thomas Wilson, both native-born Scotsmen, will not allow a slur on their countrymen. No issue is made of the objection. The offending phrase is immediately deleted.

During the reading of this final page, many changes are made. Whole sentences are taken out—those which concentrate on the treasonable qualities of the British people. Mr. Jefferson has made a strong indictment with the words:

These facts have given the last stab to agonizing affection and manly spirit bids us to renounce for- ever these unfeeling brethren. We must endeavor to forget our former love for them, and to hold them as we hold the rest of mankind, enemies in war, in peace friends. We might have been a free & a great people together; but a communication of grandeur and of freedom, it seems, is below their dignity. Be it so, since they will have it: the road to happiness and to glory is open to us too; we will climb it apart from them, and acquiesce in the necessity which denounces our eternal separation.

The delegates are convinced they must break their ties with Great Britain because of the crimes George III has committed against America. Yet, the more practical businessmen realize that eventually the new United States will want to trade with England. Thus, Mr. Jefferson's bitter charge is toned down to read:

We must, therefore, acquiesce in the necessity, which denounces our separation, and hold them, as we hold the rest of mankind, enemies in war, in peace, friends.

Years later, Thomas Jefferson, still bitter over the censoring of these phrases, would write: "The pusillanimous idea that we had friends in England worth keeping terms with, still haunted the minds of many; for this reason those passages which conveyed censures on the people of England were struck out, lest they should give them offense."

After Secretary Thomson has finished the last paragraph, a number of alterations are made. The idea of incorporating Mr. Lee's resolution into this passage seems sensible—and right. The sentences are therefore reworked to include Mr. Lee's original wording:

We, therefore, the Representatives of the United states of America in General Congress assembled, appealing to the supreme judge of the world for the rectitude of our intentions, do, in the name and by the authority of the good people of these colonies, solemnly publish and declare, that these United Colonies are, and of Right ought to be, Free and Independent States; that they are absolved from all Allegiance to the British Crown, and that all political Connection between them and the State of Great-Britain, is and ought to be totally dissolved.

. . .

Several of the delegates feel that Jefferson has been remiss in not referring more to the Almighty. The final sentence is changed to read:

And for the support of this declaration, with a firm reliance on the protection of divine providence, we mutually pledge to each other our lives, our fortunes, and our sacred honor.

Now the thing is finished. Some of the changes have been due to style. For instance, Jefferson in using the possessive pronoun "its" has always punctuated it as a contraction of "it is." Thus he has sprinkled his composition with "it's." His fellow delegates have been quick to cut out all the apostrophes.

Another of Jefferson's idiosyncracies is his belief

that capitalization has been overdone—he deplores the current practice of capitalizing nouns and verbs in the midst of sentences. As a result, he has swung to the opposite extreme, often refusing to capitalize even at the beginning of a sentence—a practice that becomes very confusing. The Congressional editors have ignored Mr. Jefferson and added many capitals throughout the document—adjectives and adverbs, as well as nouns.

Everything considered, the work of revision has been good. These delegates are men of keen minds; their alterations have not only made the Declaration a more skillful political paper, but have also improved the simplicity and force of the language. They have wisely refused to inject the issue of the slave trade into what is already a precarious situation. They have deleted all references to the English people on the grounds that it is George III alone who is responsible for the colonies' decision. In the more than eighty changes made, the text of Mr. Jefferson's paper has been reduced by almost one fourth.

Now the document stands as a concise statement of the principles upon which the new nation has been founded. Nevertheless, there is still that element of uncertainty. Will the delegates all vote "Aye" when the solemn moment arrives?

★★ *12* ★★

THE VOTE IS TAKEN

Now that the work of revision on the declaration is finished, one of the delegates requests Secretary Thomson to read the document in its final form. Once again the members of Congress, worn and weary from the long debate, listen to the now familiar opening words of the preamble. All over the room men are nodding in approval as Secretary Thomson reads: "We hold these Truths to be self-evident, that all Men are created equal, that they are endowed by their Creator with certain inalienable rights, that among these are Life, Liberty and the Pursuit of Happiness . . ."

Next comes the long list of grievances, and lastly, the actual declaration that the colonies are free and independent states, a declaration that gives no hint of the lengthy debates held before it was agreed upon, a declaration in support of which ". . . we mutually pledge to each other our Lives, our Fortunes and our sacred Honor."

With the reading of these words, the moment has arrived for the decisive step. Deep silence falls over the room, broken only by the low drone of the horse-flies buzzing through the minute openings at the top of the windows.

Secretary Thomson rises, roll book in hand and pen poised to record the final voting. According to the precedent established at the First Continental Congress two years ago, the roll call begins with the northernmost colony—New Hampshire. Josiah Bartlett, senior member of the delegation, is first and his response is a hearty "Aye." Massachusetts, Rhode Island, and Connecticut follow—all affirmatively.

Next come the Middle Colonies. The New York delegates are skipped, since they are still forbidden to vote for independence, although they announce they expect new orders any day now. Pennsylvania, New Jersey, Maryland, and Delaware add their affirmative votes.

And now the Southern colonies: Virginia, North Carolina, South Carolina, and Georgia. One by one the delegates declare themselves in favor of the Declaration. The last voice to be heard is that of the fiery little Button Gwinnett, who makes Georgia's vote unanimous with his firmly spoken "Aye."

A momentous decision has just been ratified, a decision from which there will be no retreating. These men, as representatives for the three million people of America, have declared themselves. His Majesty's colonies are now to be free and independent states. The ties with Great Britain have been severed.

Secretary Thomson reports the final tally to Chairman Harrison who then dissolves the committee of the whole. As Harrison steps down from the dais, John Hancock resumes the president's chair, once again replacing the silver mace.

In careful observance of parliamentary procedure, Chairman Harrison addresses President Hancock, reporting that "the Committee of the Whole Congress have agreed to a Declaration." The terse statement is duly recorded in the Journal of Congress.

President Hancock now reaches for the document, takes the quill pen, and dipping it into the silver inkwell on his table, affixes his signature with his customary bold flourish. Secretary Thomson also signs, not as a congressional delegate, but merely as a witness to the president's signature.

This session on July fourth has been long and wearisome. The work has consumed more time than anyone expected. The delegates would like to disperse, but there are still further details which must be discussed.

A motion is adopted that the Declaration be "authenticated and printed." Copies, it is decided, must be made up at once—tonight, if possible. Members of the Committee of Five who were originally assigned the task of drafting the Declaration are now asked to superintend its preparation. They are also given authority to make any necessary typographical corrections.

It is resolved to send a number of printed copies to General Washington by express rider, so that he may announce the proclamation to his troops as soon as possible. Further, the delegates agree to send copies to the Legislative assembly of each new state for a public reading.

There are other matters for decision, too. The desperate need for flints is again considered. General Washington never seems to have enough. And the Board of War is empowered to "employ such a number of persons, as they shall find necessary, to manufacture flints for the continent."

President Hancock reminds Congress that a seal for official documents is now a necessity. A committee is appointed, and its three members—John Adams, Thomas Jefferson, and Benjamin Franklin—are given unanimous endorsement by the delegates.

The meeting is adjourned without fanfare.

And Afterward

★★ 13 ★★

BELLS RING OUT ACROSS THE NEW NATION

Early on the evening of July 4, 1776, the Declaration was delivered to the print shop of John Dunlap on lower Market Street. The messenger who delivered the manuscript told the printer that President Hancock had said this job must be done at once, that the four pages of closely written copy should be printed as a single broadside.

Understanding the urgency of his assignment, Mr. Dunlap worked feverishly throughout the night, setting type on his handpress. By the dim glow of candlelight he followed Mr. Jefferson's intricate writing, deciphering the margin notations, trying to catch all the changes in the heavily interlined copy. Unfortunately, Mr. Dunlap was a printer who had personal whims about punctuation and capitalization. His type-setting job followed no accepted style.

Early Friday afternoon Mr. Dunlap sent the first batch of broadsides over to Secretary Thomson at the State House. The delegates snatched them up eagerly, and many wrote letters to people at home during the afternoon's proceedings, enclosing copies of the new Declaration. To a friend in Boston, John Adams explained: "I will enclose to you a Declaration in which all America is most remarkably united. It completes a revolution which will make as good a figure in the history of nations as any that has preceded it."

These first copies were all entitled "A Declaration by the Representatives of the United States of America in General Congress Assembled"—not "A Unanimous Declaration . . . ," the form familiar to us today. New York had not yet given her affirmative vote.

Secretary Thomson left a blank space in his rough Journal of Congress where he planned to insert the Declaration. Through an oversight on the part of Printer Dunlap, the manuscript from which he worked was not returned, and one of the broadsides was put into the Journal "by a wafer," a small gelatine-like disc used for attaching papers. Thus, this printed version became the first official copy.

Broadsides were dispatched immediately to Phila-

delphia's Committee of Safety; others were rushed out by postriders to the various state assemblies, but there was a lapse of several weeks before the news was known throughout the country.

On Saturday, July sixth, the Declaration first appeared in a newspaper. The Pennsylvania *Evening Post* published the document in its entirety, and for "only two copper" the citizenry could familiarize themselves with the contents of the much-discussed manuscript.

Philadelphia's Committee of Safety was put in charge of arrangements for the formal celebration, but such an important occasion necessitated several days' planning. At the top of the third page in the Monday, July eighth, issue of the *Pennsylvania Packet*, the following announcement was set in bold type:

THIS DAY, AT TWELVE O'CLOCK, THE DECLARATION OF INDEPENDENCE WILL BE PROCLAIMED AT THE STATE HOUSE.

It was decided that the State House yard would be best suited for the ceremony. The high wooden platform which supported the American Philosophical Society's observatory in the south corner could be adapted as a stage for the speaker. (Less than three weeks later this same observatory would be fitted up to house the soldiers assigned to guard the State House.)

On Monday, "a warm sunshine morning" according to the diary of a prominent Philadelphian, the
members of the committee showed up at Fifth and
Chestnut early, laden with flags to use for decoration.
These were Grand Union flags, not the Stars and
Stripes we know today. In 1776 a national flag had
not yet been designed. But the Grand Union was the
flag General Washington had chosen to display over
his headquarters outside Boston on New Year's Day.
In the upper left corner, the blue union combined two
crosses—St. George's for England and St. Andrew's
for Scotland. The field of the flag had thirteen red
and white stripes, representing the thirteen colonies.
The committee decked out the platform with small
flags, hanging the larger ones in the nearby windows
of the State House. The emblems, fluttering in the
July breeze, added an air of festivity to the usually
sedate building.

Long before the hour specified for the celebration,
people dressed in holiday attire began crowding into
the State House yard. The tall unkempt grass, seared
by the hot July sun, was soon trampled underfoot, and
thin clouds of dust swirled through the throng.

Most of the spectators were tradesmen, mechanics,
servants, apprentices who had brought their families
to hear the great proclamation read aloud. One critic
reported there were "very few respectable people"
present, a comment that can probably be attributed to

the fact that many of Philadelphia's more prosperous citizens still had Loyalist leanings.

Promptly at twelve o'clock, old Andrew MacNair, the doorman, began tugging at the rope of the great bell in the State House tower. Its booming tones electrified the city, as it rang out the news of independence. Never before had the inscription which Isaac Norris selected for the bell's rim had such meaning: "Proclaim Liberty Throughout all the Land unto all the Inhabitants Thereof." And from that day on, the bell became known as the Liberty Bell.

Members of prominent local committees were joined by the Congressional delegates as they paraded across the State House yard, accompanied by cheers from the crowd. Colonel John Nixon, a member of the Committee of Safety, mounted the steps to the platform, carrying with him a newly printed copy of the Declaration of Independence.

As Colonel Nixon unfolded the broadside, the Liberty Bell ceased ringing, and a hush fell over the spectators. In a loud clear voice he began, "A Declaration by the Representatives of the United States of America in General Congress assembled . . ."

The crowd liked the fine flow of Mr. Jefferson's language, though it is doubtful whether they comprehended all of it. But when Colonel Nixon began the long list of indictments—this was something that

everyone understood. When he had finished, the assembled spectators gave "three huzzas," adding to each cheer the words, "God bless the Free States of North America!" Immediately afterward, nine Pennsylvania soldiers, especially chosen for the honor, advanced to the State House entrance on Chestnut Street and ceremoniously removed the royal coat of arms above the door. It was hoisted into a wagon and carted down to the Old London Coffee House beside the waterfront.

During the afternoon Philadelphia's five battalions held a spirited parade on the commons, after which they stood at attention while the Declaration was again read aloud. Once it was completed, thirteen volleys were fired, volleys which John Adams reported, ". . . gave us the *feu de joie*, notwithstanding the scarcity of powder."

The joyous celebration continued throughout the day and much of the night, with bells and chimes ringing out all over the city in lusty chorus. During the evening a large crowd gathered at the Old London Coffee House, cheering with much enthusiasm as the king's coat of arms was tossed into a bonfire, and Philadelphia's symbol of royal authority disappeared in flames.

On Tuesday, July ninth, copies of the broadside reached General Washington at his headquarters in

New York City. He immediately ordered that the brigades of the Continental Army should be drawn up on the parade grounds at six o'clock, to hear the reading of the Declaration. In his directive Washington added: "The General hopes that this important event will serve as a fresh incentive to every officer and soldier to act with fidelity and courage, as knowing that now the peace and safety of his country depend, under God, solely on the success of our arms . . . ."

By late afternoon some fifteen thousand men had assembled on the commons at the lower end of Manhattan. They were an oddly clad group: no two regiments were dressed the same. Hunting shirts and buckskin breeches were predominant among the volunteers, though there was also a colorful mixture of brown, blue, and red coats. Washington's own guard wore blue coats, red vests, and buckskin breeches— by far the most presentable-looking of the entire army. Some carried rifles; others had tomahawks tucked in their belts. This was the people's army, the volunteers from sixteen to sixty who were about to face combat with too little ammunition and almost no reinforcements—all for the cause of independence.

While the troops formed on the commons, hundreds of spectators gathered in the surrounding streets, waiting to hear the reading of the Declaration. Silence fell over the crowd as a voice boomed out: "When in the course of human events . . ." The reader continued. When he reached the final phrase ". . . we mutually pledge to each other our lives, our fortunes, and our sacred honor," lusty cheers split the air.

Bonfires were lighted and some of the more spirited citizenry began tearing down nearby signs of British authority. The soldiers marched off the field to the accompaniment of fife and drum.

Meanwhile, a group of young rebels moved up Broadway until they reached Bowling Green. There the statue of George III became a challenge. Swarming over it, they began tearing down the figure of the tyrant. Some of the soldiers joined the hilarious wreckers, and it was not long before the likeness of his Majesty was broken into a thousand pieces. Justifying their assault, the young wreckers shouted they wanted the lead in the statue for Continental bullets. Eventually the scrap metal was loaded into wagons and carted off to Litchfield, Connecticut, where it was melted down for much-needed ammunition—42,550 bullets, to be precise.

General Washington deplored such riotous action and issued orders that ". . . in the future these things shall be avoided by the soldiery." The bullets were indeed helpful, but Washington could not approve the methods used to procure them.

The celebration in Boston took place at noon on

the eighteenth of July. Abigail Adams was in the tremendous crowd that gathered around the State House to listen as Colonel Thomas Crafts read the Declaration from the balcony. When he finished, the crowd began shouting "God save the American States." Abby wrote her husband that "the Bells rang, the privateers fired the forts & batteries, the cannon were discharged . . . every face appeared joyful. After dinner the King's arms were taken down from the State House . . . and burned. Thus ends royal Authority in this State and all the people shall say Amen."

As the postriders reached their destinations there were celebrations throughout the thirteen new states during that summer of 1776. From pulpits, in schoolhouses, on village greens, the Declaration was read to all America. And from a courtroom in South Carolina, Chief Justice Henry Drayton pronounced that "A new empire has arisen, styled the United States of America."

In Philadelphia's State House on the morning of July fifteenth, President Hancock read a message from the New York Assembly. The Congressmen heard the welcome news that the Assembly had found the reasons for declaring the colonies free were "cogent and conclusive." Thus the New York delegates were now finally able to cast their formal vote for the Declaration of Independence. And the title of that document was changed to the one we know today: "The Unanimous Declaration of the Thirteen United States of America."

The Journal of Congress reveals that on the nineteenth of July a resolution was affirmed ordering that "the Declaration passed on the 4th, be fairly engrossed on parchment . . . and that the same, when engrossed, be signed by every member of Congress." Timothy Matlack, a native Philadelphian and friend of Secretary Thomson, did the job in record time, so that all would be ready for August second, the date specified for the signing.

★★ *14* ★★

SIGNING THE DECLARATION, AUGUST 2, 1776

In his haste to complete the parchment for the ceremony on August second, Timothy Matlack seems to have been more concerned about the quality of his script than the accuracy of the words he was transcribing. After the document was delivered to Secretary Thomson, a number of mistakes were found.

The words "United States" in the title were written as "united States." "British" had an extra "t" added, and "only" was omitted, later to be inserted with a caret. The "en" in the word "Representative" was forgotten—and later added in the same manner. But, despite these errors, the delegates were pleased with the parchment.

Not every man who signed Timothy Matlack's engrossed parchment had voted for the Declaration.

Changes in the delegations were often made. Between July fourth and August second, a number of delegates had been replaced by new members. Thus, several gentlemen who had voted for the document were not members of Congress at the time of the signing. Nevertheless, every man present affixed his signature. A few were absent and signed afterward; when the last delegate signed—months later—the Declaration had fifty-six names on it.

On the morning of August second there was probably an air of solemn gravity in the white-paneled meeting room of the State House. Just before the signing began, William Ellery of Rhode Island walked up to the president's table and stood directly behind it, curious to watch the delegates' faces as they came forward to sign.

Some were tense, inscribing their names with obvious haste. Others wrote slowly and deliberately; theirs was a gesture of defiant pride. Later Mr. Ellery said that although he had expected to detect fear among some of the delegates, he found nothing but "dauntless resolution in every face."

President Hancock was first, and he signed in his usual large script, a signature complete with curlicues and underlinings. Legend has it that he said he wanted to make his signature large enough so that King George would not have to put on his glasses to read

it. Historians are still arguing about the authenticity of this statement, but the story has persisted. Today the phrase "John Hancock" is a synonym for a handwritten signature.

Although Secretary Charles Thomson signed the original manuscript, as a witness to President Hancock's signature, he did not sign the engrossed parchment. He was not a delegate to Congress; only Congressional delegates signed the document.

The signers came forward in thirteen separate delegations, by colonies—now states—although the states are not indicated on the document itself. New Hampshire was the first state to sign, just as it had been the first colony to vote on the issue of independence. Only two delegates were present on August second—Josiah Bartlett and William Whipple. Matthew Thornton, the third delegate from New Hampshire, could not have signed before November fourth, his first day in Congress.

Next came the men from Massachusetts, fearless and eager. After all, they represented those colonists whose ancestors had landed at Plymouth Rock in 1620—the first fugitives from England who had come to this great new land in search of freedom and justice. Theirs was an important tradition to uphold! Sam Adams was first; then came John Adams who, more than any other delegate, had struggled to make this moment a reality. And last, Robert Treat Paine. John Hancock, though a member of the Massachusetts delegation, had already inscribed his name. Elbridge Gerry was out of town on August second and added his name later.

Rhode Island's two delegates—William Ellery and Stephen Hopkins—now came forward. Next to Benjamin Franklin, Hopkins was the oldest of the delegates. He suffered from palsy and walked with the aid of a hickory cane. His handwriting was scrawling, almost illegible. As he laboriously traced his name on the parchment, he remarked to Mr. Ellery: "My hand trembles, but my heart does not."

Last in the New England group were the resolute men from Connecticut: Roger Sherman, Samuel Huntington, William Williams, and Oliver Wolcott. Roger Sherman having been a member of the committee to draft the Declaration was proud indeed to affix his signature.

The representatives from the four conservative Middle Colonies followed. Now that the New York delegates had had new instructions, all four placed their names on the parchment: William Floyd, Philip Livingston, Francis Lewis, and Lewis Morris. The men from New Jersey followed: Richard Stockton, John Witherspoon, Francis Hopkinson, John Hart, and Abraham Clark.

Caesar Rodney was the first to sign for Delaware, followed by George Read. Although Read had voted against the adoption of Mr. Lee's resolution on July second, he was present to affix his signature on the morning of August second. Thomas McKean was absent, probably because of ill health. An authenticated list of signers was printed by order of Congress on January 18, 1777, and at that time there were only fifty-five signatures, so it must be presumed that some time after that date McKean signed.

Now it was Pennsylvania's turn. Robert Morris, although he had absented himself from Congress on the day Mr. Lee's resolution was adopted, signed the document. John Morton and James Wilson, who had both supported independence, affixed their signatures. Benjamin Rush, George Clymer, James Smith, George Taylor, and George Ross were all newcomers, having been elected as delegates from Pennsylvania on July twentieth, some sixteen days after the issue of independence was settled. However, they all signed eagerly.

Another legend is often repeated about the moment when Dr. Franklin limped up to the president's table. As the old gentleman peered at the document through his small-lensed spectacles, President Hancock is supposed to have tried to hurry the good doctor. "Come, come. We must be Unanimous. We must all hang

together," urged the president. To which the wise old sage of Philadelphia is purported to have replied, "Indeed, we must all hang together. Otherwise, we shall most assuredly all hang separately." Whether this story is true is open to question, but it is indeed characteristic of Benjamin Franklin's wisdom and dry humor.

The name of John Dickinson, the once prominent leader of the Pennsylvania delegation, does not appear on the document. He was not eligible to sign, for he had been replaced as a delegate to Congress. Many people persisted in calling him a Tory, but Dickinson ignored the charge and fought valiantly under General Washington's command throughout the Revolutionary War.

From Maryland the signers were Samuel Chase, William Paca, Thomas Stone, and Charles Carroll. The story is told that after Charles Carroll had signed his name, one of the delegates remarked that Mr. Carroll wasn't taking too much of a risk, because there were several men by that same name residing in Maryland. Hearing this comment, Carroll promptly added "of Carrollton" so that he could be readily identified. (He is the only signer who included his address on the roster.)

Virginia had seven signers although on Monday, August second, only five were present: Thomas Jefferson, Benjamin Harrison, Thomas Nelson, Jr., Francis Lightfoot Lee, and Carter Braxton. Richard Henry Lee, who had first proposed the resolution for independence, and George Wythe were both in Williamsburg and had to sign the Declaration at a later date.

William Hooper, Joseph Hewes, and John Penn signed for North Carolina; Edward Rutledge, Thomas Heyward, Jr., Thomas Lynch, Jr., and Arthur Middleton for South Carolina. Youngest of the thirteen colonies was Georgia; the three Georgia signers were Button Gwinnett, Lyman Hall, and George Walton.

The scene in the State House on that memorable August second must have been very similar to the one portrayed by the artist John Trumbull several years later. No visitor, of course, was allowed in the white-paneled chamber during the signing, but Trumbull visited the room many times afterward, studying the setting and asking various members of Congress to pose for him. It is interesting to note that in the painting Thomas Jefferson looks far more mature than his thirty-three years would indicate. This is explained by the fact that he did not pose for Trumbull until ten years later, while residing in Paris.

The fifty-six signers were men of varied talents, representing a broad cross-section of colonial life. Some were self-made men who had come from humble homes; others were well educated, wealthy, cultivated. But they all had one denominator in common—they had been leaders in the colonies which elected them. All had a vital interest in public affairs.

More than half of the signers were lawyers; however, many of them did not practice professionally. The majority of the Southern delegates were plantation owners. The group included four physicians, although only Dr. Benjamin Rush carried on active practice. The one clergyman, Dr. John Witherspoon, was president of the College at Princeton. Francis Hopkinson had the distinction of being the only composer and poet. (It was Hopkinson who later designed the United States flag for General Washington.)

Robert Morris and Philip Livingston had both made large fortunes as merchants. John Hancock had inherited a sizable sum of money. And Charles Carroll of Carrollton was reputed to be the wealthiest man in America.

Most of the signers had been born in either the American colonies or the British Isles. They had been reared with a strong sense of loyalty to British institutions. More than half were college graduates or had studied in Europe. With the exception of Charles Carroll (who was a Roman Catholic), all the signers were Protestant in religion. Edward Rutledge of South Carolina was the youngest delegate, being twenty-six when he signed the Declaration; Benjamin Franklin, at seventy, was the oldest, but the majority of signers were in their thirties or forties, intellectually mature in their judgments.

Whatever their backgrounds, the signers were men of vision who had endorsed the boldest of courses—to declare thirteen colonies a free and independent nation. By signing the parchment, they were risking their lives, their families, and their fortunes for the cause of liberty.

The price these brave men paid was high. Almost every signer suffered hardships and financial losses in the Revolutionary War. Afterward, some slipped into obscurity; others rose to prominence in the newly formed government, and their works have become familiar to every student of history.

In the early summer of 1826, extensive plans were made throughout the nation for celebrating the fiftieth anniversary of the adoption of the Declaration of Independence. Eighty-three-year-old Thomas Jefferson was gravely ill at Monticello, but he clung tenaciously to life until the early morning hours of July fourth. Several hundred miles north, at his home in Quincy, Massachusetts, ninety-year-old John Adams died less than two hours after death came to Jefferson.

When the news spread through the nation, people were filled with both sorrow and wonder—that two

Presidents of the United States, the author and the stoutest defender of the Declaration of Independence should die within hours of each other—and on the fiftieth anniversary of the document's adoption! It was an amazing coincidence, probably without parallel in history.

★★ *15* ★★

TRAVELS OF A PARCHMENT

The broadside, printed by Mr. Dunlap in the early morning hours of July fifth, was the official copy of the Declaration which was attached to the rough Journal of Congress. There is no indication that this paper was treated with any particular care. However, after Timothy Matlack had engrossed the composition on parchment, and it had been signed by all the members of Congress present, it is probable that the document began to take on new importance. Secretary Thomson kept the parchment rolled up and brought it out only when a delegate needed to add his signature.

Toward the end of 1776, the British were advancing toward Philadelphia. An alarmed Congress decided to

move to Baltimore. The Declaration, along with all
the other Congressional papers, was transported in a
light wagon. It was in Baltimore that the document
was printed again, and for the first time, the names of
the various signers were made public.

Although Congress returned to Philadelphia in the
spring of 1777, it was forced to flee again in the fall—
this time to Lancaster and then to York, Pennsylvania,
where the Declaration was stored in the courthouse.

By July 4, 1778, Congress had returned to Philadelphia, and the parchment remained in the State House
until July 1783. More traveling followed as Congress
moved to Princeton, to Trenton, to Annapolis, and
finally to New York City in June 1785. There the
Declaration was stored in the City Hall on Wall
Street, and when General Washington was inaugu-
rated as President in 1789, the precious document was
placed in the custody of the acting Secretary of State,
John Jay.

After Thomas Jefferson became Secretary of State
under President Washington, the paper which he had
drafted came into his possession. From 1790 until
1800, the government had its headquarters once again
in Philadelphia. The Declaration was kept first at a
building on Market Street and later taken to the State
House.

Meanwhile, President Washington's dream of creat-

ing a new Federal capital had begun to assume reality.
By the fall of 1800, the government was moving to
Washington, D.C., and the Declaration was transported there, with more than usual care. For the next
fourteen years it was stored in the War Office Building
on Seventeenth Street.

In mid-August of 1814, the invasion of Washington
by British soldiers seemed imminent. Secretary of
State James Monroe hurriedly packed up the papers
of his office, including the Declaration, in a linen sack,
and the sack was placed for one night in Edgar Patter-
son's barn, about two miles from Chain Bridge, Virginia. The next day the sack was taken to the home of
the Reverend Littlejohn at Leesburg, and there it
remained for several weeks.

Fortunately, the British made a hasty retreat after
setting fire to the Executive Mansion on August
twenty-fourth. Within a month, the precious papers
were returned to Washington and placed in the building occupied by the State Department.

By now the general public was becoming more
aware of the importance of the Declaration. An enter-
prising penman, Benjamin Owen Tyler, copied the
document, and in 1818 the first engravings of it were
published. So meticulous was Mr. Tyler in reproduc-
ing the signatures of the signers that Richard Rush,
then Secretary of State, found them "curiously exact,"

almost impossible to distinguish from the originals. (And Secretary Rush's father, Benjamin, had been one of the signers.)

The following year John Binns, publisher of the *Democratic Press* in Philadelphia, issued a facsimile, complete with seals of the states and illustrated with pictures of Washington, Hancock, and Jefferson. The fact that George Washington was commanding troops in New York City when the Declaration was signed, and that our first President was not a signer, did not seem to bother the purchasers of Mr. Binns's copy. These reproductions were a commercial venture but nevertheless proved very successful.

In 1823 the Secretary of State, John Quincy Adams, ordered that an official facsimile be made. The Declaration was first dusted with powder. Then moist printing paper was applied to the parchment, and an exact copy was lifted from the original. Today experts believe that the making of this facsimile caused some of the ink to be loosened, especially on the signatures. Copies were distributed throughout the country, and the Declaration soon became a familiar sight.

During these years the parchment was always rolled up for storage—never folded. The difference in legibility of the various signatures may be attributed to several factors. All signers did not use the same pen, nor the same kind of ink. They did not all sign on the

same day, either. Furthermore, ink does not sink into parchment as it does into paper, and once the ink dries, it flakes off more easily. Because the Declaration was always rolled from bottom to top, the lower signatures were those injured most.

By 1841 a new, white marble building for the Patent Office was completed at Seventh and F Streets. Since the structure was believed to be fireproof, Secretary of State Daniel Webster suggested to Henry L. Ellsworth, Commissioner of Patents, that this new building would be an appropriate place in which to display historic documents. Within a few months one room was designated as "the National Gallery," and the Declaration was framed with General Washington's commission as Commander in Chief as a single exhibit.

The two documents hung opposite a window, which exposed them to "the chill of winter and the glare and heat of summer." There the Declaration remained for thirty-five years, the parchment yellowing in the constant light. Writers during this time referred to the document as "that old-looking paper," and occasionally expressed surprise that nothing was done to preserve such a famous manuscript.

When the Centennial was held in Philadelphia in 1876, the document was once again transported to its original birthplace. But by this time many of the signatures had faded out, and the text, although legible, had become quite dim. For purposes of exhibition, the document was placed in a fireproof safe behind a plate-glass door. Among the thousands who gazed through the glass, there was surprised wonder and, more often, concern about the visible deterioration of such a venerable paper.

Despite the efforts of many Philadelphia residents to keep the Declaration in their city, the United States Government insisted that it be brought back to Washington. The Department of State had moved into a new fireproof building, and fortunately the Declaration was taken there for display—fortunately because within a few months the Patent Office Building went up in flames. At the State Department, the Declaration was placed in a cabinet in the library, remaining there on exhibition for the next seventeen years.

In 1894 government officials became alarmed at the condition of the parchment, and the Secretary of State ordered that the Declaration be "sealed between two sheets of glass, presumably proof against air, and locked in a steel safe." Some suggested that chemicals be used; others felt that keeping it away from heat and light would be the best restorative. And for the next twenty-six years, no one was allowed to see the Declaration, except by special permission of the Secretary of State.

In 1920 a committee of experts was appointed to examine the Declaration and make recommendations for its preservation. After extensive research, the committee concluded that the Declaration could once again be exhibited, provided it was "hermetically sealed between sheets of glass and exposed only to diffused light."

At the suggestion of Secretary of State Charles Evans Hughes, President Harding issued an order that the Library of Congress should take over the care and preservation of the document. On September 30, 1921, it was transported to Capitol Hill in one of the Library's mail wagons and placed in a safe in the office of the Librarian, Dr. Herbert Putnam.

Within a few months Congress voted an appropriation for the building of "a sort of shrine" in which the Declaration and the Constitution would permanently be housed. Francis H. Bacon (brother of the man who designed the Lincoln Memorial) was the architect. He designed an upright case with bronze doors for the Declaration and a desklike case for the

Constitution. Both cases were covered with double panes of plate glass and specially prepared sheets of gelatin film were inserted to filter out harmful light rays.

On February 28, 1924, the shrine was dedicated. President and Mrs. Calvin Coolidge, along with a representative group from Congress, watched as Dr. Putnam placed both the Declaration and the Constitution in their respective cases, closed the lids, and turned the locks. Uniformed guards were placed on duty around the clock to see that no harm was done to the treasured documents.

When the Japanese attacked Pearl Harbor on December 7, 1941, the Librarian became alarmed about the safety of the Declaration and the Constitution. On the day before Christmas they were removed from the shrine and placed in a specially designed bronze container. On December twenty-sixth the container was loaded into an armored truck and taken to Union Station, accompanied by a detail of Secret Service men. There the cargo was placed in a compartment on a train bound for Louisville, guarded by the Secret Service. Upon arrival in Kentucky the following morning, an armored truck and a regiment of soldiers accompanied the container to a vault at Fort Knox.

While the Declaration was stored at Fort Knox, it was occasionally taken out and examined by experts.

Under controlled atmospheric conditions, several repairs were made, including the drawing together of wide cracks in the parchment.

By the fall of 1944, the military authorities concluded that any wartime danger to the Library of Congress had ended, and the bronze container was returned from its vault in Kentucky. Once again the documents were installed where visitors might see them in the shrine of the Library of Congress.

After the National Archives Building was completed, it was decided to place both the Declaration and the Constitution in the Exhibition Hall, along with other valuable state papers. The move from the Library of Congress to the new National Archives Building was conducted with elaborate ceremony. On December 12, 1952, guards from all the armed services carried the containers down the library steps and placed them in an armored tank. Escorted by service men and women, the tank rolled down Pennsylvania Avenue until it reached the new depository.

The unveiling of the new shrine took place on December 15, 1952. The Chief Justice of the Supreme Court presided at the ceremony, and President Truman delivered an address to a large group of dignitaries.

Sealed in bronze-and-glass cases filled with helium, the documents today are protected by special filters.

Guards stand a twenty-four-hour watch, and should there be need, both documents can be lowered into a large fireproof and shockproof case at a moment's notice.

Thousands of visitors throng into the Exhibition Hall each year to gaze in awe at the Declaration of Independence and the Constitution of the United States. In the words of Archibald MacLeish, a former Librarian of Congress, "Nothing that men have ever made surpasses them."

★★ *16* ★★

THE DECLARATION, THEN AND NOW

The Declaration of Independence was the world's first document to set forth the ideals of democracy. It is unique in that it was conceived by thought rather than violence. No other colony in history had ever attempted to break from the mother country through force of logic rather than the impact of ammunition.

In a letter to Henry Lee, Jr., written on May 8, 1825, the elderly Mr. Jefferson wrote that his purpose in framing the Declaration was "not to find out new principles or new arguments, never before thought of; not merely to say things which had never been said before; but to place before mankind the common sense of the subject. . . . Neither aiming at originality of principle or sentiment, nor yet copied from any particular and previous writing, it was intended to be an expression of the American mind, and to give that expression the proper tone and spirit called for by the occasion."

Unlike the Constitution of the United States, formulated in 1787, the Declaration of Independence does not specify how we shall be governed. Mr. Jefferson's manuscript was basically an expression of political principles upon which this republic could be founded.

By adopting the Declaration, the delegates to the Second Continental Congress committed the new nation to these principles. Although written by an American for America, the fundamentals expressed have achieved world-wide acceptance by all people who believe in democracy.

As a piece of literature, the Declaration ranks among the world's great writings. As a state paper, embodying the political philosophy of a new nation, Thomas Jefferson's composition stands alone. No other country has ever produced such a document.

The story is told that many years after the Declaration was adopted, a visitor called at the home of the Marquis de Lafayette. On the wall of his library was a handsomely framed engraving of the original facsimile of the Declaration. Beside it was a matching frame with nothing in it. When the visitor remarked about the unusual exhibit, Lafayette explained, "I am waiting for France to do the same!"

It is interesting to note that the name by which we know this venerable document—"The Declaration of Independence"—appears nowhere in the paper itself, in either the title or the text. Mr. Jefferson's rough draft reveals that he began to write "A Declaration of," then crossed out the word "of," and substituted "by," thus entitling the document: "A Declaration by the Representatives of the United States of America, in General Congress assembled." Why the author made this change will never be known. Historians believe that it was probably because Mr. Jefferson felt that the document should also include a basic philosophy of government, a statement that would be more inclusive than the mere severing of ties with Great Britain.

During the summer of 1776 when the Declaration was being read and discussed throughout the thirteen new states, the people were most interested in the final paragraphs. These were the crux of the action which had been taken; they read and reread the crucial words.

The preamble and the second paragraph caused little comment. The language was impressive, and it was expected that the words would be somewhat flowery. This was the accepted mode of writing in the eighteenth century. However, political philosophy was a subject studied by the intellectuals. The man on the street wanted specifics. The list of grievances, the ac-

tual charges against George III, proved far more interesting.

Today, however, the emphasis is quite different. As
Americans, we have enjoyed independence for so many
years that the later paragraphs containing detailed
reasons for severing the ties with England no longer
hold the importance they did for the early American
citizen. The grievances listed are, for the most part,
local matters pertinent only to the late eighteenth
century. At the present time only a reader who knows
colonial history can understand in detail the significance of the charges.

The universal appeal of the Declaration lies in the
philosophical second paragraph, the "why" of the
Declaration. In his opening sentences, Mr. Jefferson
expressed a philosophy which is timeless—that all
men are created equal . . . that it is the right and
privilege of men to live in freedom and pursue happiness with a government of their own choosing . . .
that this government shall make its laws only with the
consent of the governed . . . that there shall be equal
opportunity and justice for each individual.

For almost two hundred years tribute and praise
have been heaped upon the Declaration, but perhaps
none has been more eloquent than that expressed by
Abraham Lincoln. During his inaugural journey to
Washington in 1861, Mr. Lincoln stopped in Phila-

delphia for a brief visit. Speaking in Independence Hall on George Washington's birthday, he said:

> . . . I have never had a feeling politically that did not spring from the sentiments embodied in the Declaration of Independence. I have often pondered over the dangers which were incurred by the men who assembled here, and framed and adopted the Declaration of Independence. I have pondered over the toils that were endured by the officers and soldiers of the army who achieved that Independence. I have often inquired of myself what great principle or idea it was that kept this Confederacy so long together. It was not the mere matter of the separation of the Colonies from the motherland; but that sentiment in the Declaration of Independence which gave liberty, not alone to the people of this country, but, I hope to the world, for all future time . . .

The text of the Declaration of Independence now in the National Archives Building in Washington, D.C.

IN CONGRESS, JULY 4, 1776

THE UNANIMOUS DECLARATION
OF THE THIRTEEN UNITED STATES OF AMERICA

When in the Course of human Events, it becomes necessary for one People to dissolve the Political Bands which have connected them with another, and to assume among the Powers of the Earth, the separate and equal Station to which the Laws of Nature and of Nature's God entitle them, a decent Respect to the Opinions of Mankind requires that they should declare the causes which impel them to the Separation.

We hold these Truths to be self-evident, that all Men are created equal, that they are endowed by their Creator with certain unalienable Rights, that among these are Life, Liberty, and the Pursuit of Happiness —That to secure these Rights, Governments are instituted among Men, deriving their just Powers from the Consent of the Governed, that whenever any Form of Government becomes destructive of these

Ends, it is the Right of the People to alter or to abolish it, and to institute new Government, laying its Foundation on such Principles, and organizing its Powers in such Form, as to them shall seem most likely to effect their Safety and Happiness. Prudence, indeed, will dictate that Governments long established should not be changed for light and transient Causes; and accordingly all Experience hath shewn, that Mankind are more disposed to suffer, while Evils are sufferable, than to right themselves by abolishing the Forms to which they are accustomed. But when a long Train of Abuses and Usurpations, pursuing invariably the same Object, evinces a Design to reduce them under absolute Despotism, it is their Right, it is their Duty, to throw off such Government, and to provide new Guards for their future Security. Such has been the patient Sufferance of these Colonies; and such is now the Necessity which constrains them to alter their former Systems of Government. The History of the present King of Great-Britain is a History of repeated Injuries and Usurpations, all having in direct Object the Establishment of an absolute Tyranny over these States. To prove this, let Facts be submitted to a candid World.

He has refused his Assent to Laws, the most wholesome and necessary for the public Good.

He has forbidden his Governors to pass Laws of immediate and pressing Importance, unless suspended in their Operation till his Assent should be obtained; and when so suspended, he has utterly neglected to attend to them.

HE has refused to pass other Laws for the Accommodation of large Districts of People, unless those People would relinquish the Right of Representation in the Legislature, a Right inestimable to them, and formidable to Tyrants only.

HE has called together Legislative Bodies at Places unusual, uncomfortable, and distant from the Depository of their public Records, for the sole Purpose of fatiguing them into Compliance with his Measures.

HE has dissolved Representative Houses repeatedly, for opposing with manly Firmness his Invasions on the Rights of the People.

HE has refused for a long Time, after such Dissolutions, to cause others to be elected; whereby the Legislative Powers, incapable of Annihilation, have returned to the People at large for their exercise; the State remaining in the mean time exposed to all the Dangers of Invasion from without, and Convulsions within.

HE has endeavoured to prevent the Population of these States; for that Purpose obstructing the Laws for Naturalization of Foreigners; refusing to pass others to encourage their Migrations hither, and raising the Conditions of new Appropriations of Lands.

HE has obstructed the Administration of Justice, by

refusing his Assent to Laws for establishing Judiciary Powers.

He has made Judges dependent on his Will alone, for the Tenure of their Offices, and the Amount and Payment of their Salaries.

He has erected a Multitude of new Offices, and sent hither Swarms of Officers to harrass our People, and eat out their Substance.

He has kept among us, in Times of Peace, Standing Armies, without the consent of our Legislatures.

He has affected to render the Military independent of and superior to the Civil Power.

He has combined with others to subject us to a Jurisdiction foreign to our Constitution, and unacknowledged by our Laws; giving his Assent to their Acts of pretended Legislation:

For quartering large Bodies of Armed Troops among us:

For protecting them, by a mock Trial, from Punishment for any Murders which they should commit on the Inhabitants of these States:

For cutting off our Trade with all Parts of the World:

For imposing Taxes on us without our Consent:

For depriving us, in many Cases, of the Benefits of Trial by Jury:

For transporting us beyond Seas to be tried for pretended Offences:

For abolishing the free System of English Laws in a neighbouring Province, establishing therein an arbitrary Government, and enlarging its Boundaries, so as to render it at once an Example and fit Instrument for introducing the same absolute Rule into these Colonies:

For taking away our Charters, abolishing our most valuable Laws, and altering fundamentally the Forms of our Governments:

For suspending our own Legislatures, and declaring themselves invested with Power to legislate for us in all Cases whatsoever.

He has abdicated Government here, by declaring us out of his Protection and waging War against us.

He has plundered our Seas, ravaged our Coasts, burnt our Towns, and destroyed the Lives of our People.

He is, at this Time, transporting large Armies of foreign Mercenaries to compleat the Works of Death, Desolation, and Tyranny, already begun with circumstances of Cruelty and Perfidy, scarcely paralleled in the most barbarous Ages, and totally unworthy the Head of a civilized Nation.

He has constrained our fellow Citizens taken Captive on the high Seas to bear Arms against their Country, to become the Executioners of their Friends and Brethren, or to fall themselves by their Hands.

He has excited domestic Insurrections amongst us,

and has endeavoured to bring on the Inhabitants of our Frontiers, the merciless Indian Savages, whose known Rule of Warfare, is an undistinguished Destruction, of all Ages, Sexes and Conditions.

In every stage of these Oppressions we have Petitioned for Redress in the most humble Terms: Our repeated Petitions have been answered only by repeated Injury. A Prince, whose Character is thus marked by every act which may define a Tyrant, is unfit to be the Ruler of a free People.

Nor have we been wanting in Attentions to our British Brethren. We have warned them from Time to Time of Attempts by their Legislature to extend an unwarrantable Jurisdiction over us. We have reminded them of the Circumstances of our Emigration and Settlement here. We have appealed to their native Justice and Magnanimity, and we have conjured them by the Ties of our common Kindred to disavow these Usurpations, which, would inevitably interrupt our Connections and Correspondence. They too have been deaf to the Voice of Justice and of Consanguinity. We must, therefore, acquiesce in the Necessity, which denounces our Separation, and hold them, as we hold the rest of Mankind, Enemies in War, in Peace, Friends.

We, therefore, the Representatives of the UNITED STATES OF AMERICA, in GENERAL

CONGRESS, Assembled, appealing to the Supreme Judge of the World for the Rectitude of our Intentions, do, in the Name, and by the Authority of the good People of these Colonies, solemnly Publish and Declare, That these United Colonies are, and of Right ought to be, FREE AND INDEPENDENT STATES; that they are absolved from all Allegiance to the British Crown, and that all political Connection between them and the State of Great-Britain, is and ought to be totally dissolved; and that as FREE AND INDEPENDENT STATES, they have full Power to levy War, conclude Peace, contract Alliances, establish Commerce, and to do all other Acts and Things which INDEPENDENT STATES may of right do. And for the support of this Declaration, with a firm Reliance on the Protection of divine Providence, we mutually pledge to each other our Lives, our Fortunes, and our sacred Honor.

JOHN HANCOCK

New Hampshire
  Josiah Bartlett
  Wm Whipple
  Matthew Thornton

Massachusetts
  Saml Adams
  John Adams
  Robt Treat Paine

Elbridge Gerry
Rhode Island
  Step. Hopkins
  William Ellery

Connecticut
  Roger Sherman
  Saml Huntington
  Wm Williams
  Oliver Wolcott

New York
  W^M FLOYD
  PHIL. LIVINGSTON
  FRAN^S LEWIS
  LEWIS MORRIS

New Jersey
  RICH^D STOCKTON
  J^{NO} WITHERSPOON
  FRA^S HOPKINSON
  JOHN HART
  ABRA CLARK

Delaware
  CAESAR RODNEY
  GEO READ
  THO M'KEAN

Pennsylvania
  ROB^T MORRIS
  BENJAMIN RUSH
  BENJ^A FRANKLIN
  JOHN MORTON
  GEO CLYMER
  JA^S SMITH
  GEO. TAYLOR
  JAMES WILSON
  GEO. ROSS

Maryland
  SAMUEL CHASE
  W^M PACA
  THO^S STONE
  CHARLES CARROLL
    OF CARROLLTON

Virginia
  GEORGE WYTHE
  RICHARD HENRY LEE
  TH JEFFERSON
  BENJ^A HARRISON
  THO^S NELSON JR.
  FRANCIS LIGHTFOOT LEE
  CARTER BRAXTON

North Carolina
  W^M HOOPER
  JOSEPH HEWES
  JOHN PENN

South Carolina
  EDWARD RUTLEDGE
  THO^S HEYWARD JUN^R
  THOMAS LYNCH JUN^R
  ARTHUR MIDDLETON

Georgia
  BUTTON GWINNETT
  LYMAN HALL
  GEO WALTON

BIBLIOGRAPHY

ADAMS, CHARLES FRANCIS. *Familiar Letters of John Adams*. Cambridge: Riverside Press, 1876.

ADAMS, JAMES TRUSLOW. *The Adams Family*. Boston: Little, Brown & Company, 1930.

ALLEN, HERBERT S. *John Hancock: Patriot in Purple*. New York: Macmillan, 1948.

AMERICAN HERITAGE, Editors of. *Let Freedom Ring: The Story of Independence Hall*. New York: American Heritage Publishing Company, 1962.

BECKER, CARL. *The Declaration of Independence: A Study in the History of Political Ideas*. New York: Alfred A. Knopf, 1942.

BOWEN, CATHERINE DRINKER. *John Adams and the American Revolution*. Boston: Little, Brown & Company, 1950.

BOYD, JULIAN P. *The Declaration of Independence: The Evolution of the Text.* Princeton, New Jersey: Princeton University Press, 1945.

BRIDENBAUGH, CARL. *Cities in Revolt.* New York: Alfred A. Knopf, 1955.

BURNETT, EDMUND C. *The Continental Congress.* New York: The Macmillan Company, 1941.

BURNETT, EDMUND C., Editor. *Letters of Members of the Continental Congress.* 8 volumes. Washington, D.C.: Carnegie Institute of Washington, 1921–36.

BURT, STRUTHERS. *Philadelphia: Holy Experiment.* Garden City, New York: Doubleday, Doran & Company, 1945.

CHIDSEY, DONALD BARR. *July 4, 1776.* New York: Crown Publishers, Inc., 1958.

DONOVAN, FRANK. *The Thomas Jefferson Papers.* New York: Dodd, Mead & Company, 1963.

DOS PASSOS, JOHN. *The Men Who Made the Nation.* New York: Doubleday & Company, 1957.

DOWNS, ROBERT B. *Books That Changed the World.* Chicago: American Library Association, 1956.

DUMBAULD, EDWARD. *The Declaration of Independence and What It Means Today.* Norman, Oklahoma: University of Oklahoma Press, 1950.

EBERLEIN, HAROLD and CORTLANDT HUBBARD. *Diary of Independence Hall.* Philadelphia: J. B. Lippincott, 1948.

ECKMAN, JEANNETTE. *Delaware: A Guide to the First State*. New York: Hastings House, 1955.

FORD, WORTHINGTON C., Editor. *Journals of the Continental Congress, 1774–1789*. Washington, D.C.: Government Printing Office, 1904–1937.

FRENCH, ALLEN. *The First Year of the American Revolution*. Boston: Houghton Mifflin Company, 1934.

GIPSON, LAWRENCE HENRY. *The Coming of the American Revolution, 1763–1775*. New York: Harper & Brothers, 1954.

HAWKE, DAVID. *A Transaction of Free Men: The Birth and Course of the Declaration of Independence*. New York: Charles Scribner's Sons, 1964.

HIRST, FRANCIS W. *Life and Letters of Thomas Jefferson*. New York: The Macmillan Company, 1926.

KIMBALL, MARIE. *Jefferson: The Road to Glory, 1743 to 1776*. New York: Coward-McCann, Inc., 1943.

LANCASTER, BRUCE. *From Lexington to Liberty*. Garden City, New York: Doubleday & Company, 1955.

LENGYEL, CORNEL. *Four Days in July*. Garden City, New York: Doubleday & Company, 1958.

McGEE, DOROTHY HORTON. *Famous Signers of the Declaration*. New York: Dodd, Mead & Company, 1955.

MALONE, DUMAS. *Jefferson the Virginian*. Boston: Little, Brown & Company, 1948.

————. *The Story of the Declaration of Independence*. New York: Oxford University Press, 1954.

MEARNS, DAVID C. *The Declaration of Independence: The Story of a Parchment*. Washington, D.C.: Library of Congress, 1950.

MEIGS, CORNELIA. *The Violent Men*. New York: The Macmillan Company, 1949.

MILLER, JOHN C. *Origins of the American Revolution*. Boston: Little, Brown & Company, 1943.

————. *Sam Adams*. Boston: Little, Brown & Company, 1936.

MONTROSS, LYNN. *The Reluctant Rebels*. New York: Harper and Brothers, 1950.

MORRIS, RICHARD B., Editor. *The Era of the American Revolution*. New York: Columbia University Press, 1939.

NEALE, OSCAR W. *World-famous Pictures*. Chicago: Lyons and Carnahan, 1933.

POWELL, JOHN H., Editor. "Speech of John Dickinson," *Pennsylvania Magazine of History and Biography*. Volume LXV, October, 1941. Pages 468–481.

QUAIFE, MILO. *The History of the United States Flag*. New York: Harper & Brothers, 1961.

RAWSON, JONATHAN. *1776: A Day-by-Day Story*. New York: Frederick A. Stokes, 1927.

ROGERS, FRANCES and ALICE BEARD. *Old Liberty Bell*. Philadelphia: Frederick A. Stokes Company, 1942.

ROSEWATER, VICTOR. *The Liberty Bell: Its History and Significance*. New York: D. Appleton & Company, 1926.

ROSSITER, CLINTON. *Seedtime of the Republic*. New York: Harcourt, Brace & Company, 1953.

SCHACHNER, NATHAN. *Thomas Jefferson: A Biography*. 2 volumes. New York: Appleton-Century-Crofts, Inc., 1951.

SINCLAIR, MERLE and ANNABEL DOUGLAS MC-ARTHUR. *They Signed for Us*. New York: Duell, Sloan & Pearce, 1957.

SINGLETON, ESTHER. *Historic Buildings of America*. New York: Dodd, Mead, and Company, 1907.

SMITH, PAGE. *John Adams*. 2 volumes. New York: Doubleday & Company, 1962.

STILLE, CHARLES J. *The Life and Times of John Dickinson, 1732–1808*. Philadelphia: Historical Society of Pennsylvania, 1891.

STONE, IRVING. *Those Who Love: A Biographical Novel of Abigail and John Adams*. Garden City, New York. Doubleday & Company, 1965.

WELCH, EARL. *Cradle of Our Nation: Philadelphia*. New York: Henry Holt and Company, 1949.

WHITNEY, DAVID C. *Founders of Freedom in America*. Chicago: J. G. Ferguson, 1964.

WRITERS' PROGRAM. *Pennsylvania: A Guide to the Keystone State*. New York: Oxford University Press, 1940.

INDEX

ABOUT THE AUTHOR

Mary Kay Phelan regards historical research as both a vocation and an avocation. She does research for and edits 8-mm. historical movies. She has written three books in the Crowell Holiday series: *Mother's Day*, *The Fourth of July*, and *Election Day*.

Mrs. Phelan was born in Baldwin City, Kansas. She was graduated from DePauw University in Greencastle, Indiana, and received her M.A. from Northwestern University. She lives with her family in Davenport, Iowa.

ABOUT THE ARTIST

Charles Walker was graduated cum laude from Syracuse University where he received a B.F.A. degree. He attended the Art Students League and studied with John Groth and Joseph Hirsch. Mr. Walker was awarded the Western Writers of America Cover Art Award. He has illustrated many children's books, and his work has appeared in *Harper's*, *Horizon*, and *Good Housekeeping* magazines. Mr. Walker enjoys classical music and the theater. He lives in Roosevelt, New York, with his wife and six children.